SAVOR

13-Digit ISBN: 978-1-60433-823-2
10-Digit ISBN: 1-60433-823-7

This book may be ordered by mail from the publisher. Please include $5.99 for postage and handling.
Please support your local bookseller first!

Books published by Cider Mill Press Book Publishers are available at special discounts for bulk purchases in the United States by corporations, institutions, and other organizations. For more information, please contact the publisher.

Cider Mill Press Book Publishers
"Where good books are ready for press"
PO Box 454
12 Spring Street
Kennebunkport, Maine 04046

Visit us online!
cidermillpress.com

Typography: Adobe Garamond Pro and Gotham
Image Credits: Page 272

Printed in China
8 9 10 11 12 13 14 15

SAVOR

Entertaining with Charcuterie,
Cheese, Spreads & More

KIMBERLY STEVENS

CIDER MILL PRESS

BOOK PUBLISHERS
KENNEBUNKPORT, MAINE

TABLE *of* CONTENTS

❧

INTRODUCTION:
A MOVABLE FEAST

When the serving board comes out, it means something special is about to happen. It seems impossible, but that humble wooden board can easily become the most extravagant serving piece at a table. Its ability to mirror the mood of a host and transform a room's ambiance renders a standard plate boring and ineffectual.

Whether it is a gorgeous assortment of hard-to-obtain cheeses for a formal dinner party, or a simple afternoon nibble of nuts and sliced fruit to go with a chilled glass of Rosé, serving anything on a board instantly elevates the moment. Large or small, round or rectangular, unfinished or polished, a board can take many forms. But no matter what, it is always a welcome sight.

Traditionally, it is used to showcase something beautiful: a few perfect tomatoes from the garden, a wedge of cheese recommended by a local cheese monger, or a luxurious pile of cured meat. Whether it is presenting these, a loaf of bread fresh from the oven, olives a friend brought back from their travels, or a beautiful handmade preserve and a handful of crackers you baked yourself, the serving board is a blank canvas, made to let you craft, slice, and display limitless combinations of foodstuffs that suit your tastes and moods.

After speaking with so many experts with opinions about the perfect board, everyone was in full agreement that the board itself is the foundation of greatness, no matter what form it may take. It always has a couple of great stories to tell: the contents sum up the party, and its scarred surface relates the snacks and meals gone by. Just looking at a certain stain or knife mark brings the memories rushing back. Most importantly, a beautiful board always leads to conversation, which is what we're all after, in the end.

SAVOR THE SERVING BOARD:
BLACKCREEK MERCANTILE & TRADING CO.

❧

Joshua Vogel has been a woodworker his whole life and owns Blackcreek Mercantile & Trading Co., located in Kingston, New York. He specializes in making furniture, as well as a collection of smaller handmade goods, including serving boards.

❧

"Think of all of the places that serving boards pop up in advertising and marketing," said Vogel. "Watch food ads on television, especially fast food ads. Eight out of 10 times there will be some wooden cutting board in the presentation shot. Keep an eye out, you will see. I don't think about it as merely a gimmick, there is something very deep-seated, some familiar connection, a chord that is struck that they are using to communicate some inherent message to you. Not only is it culturally ingrained, it is cross-culturally ingrained within us. It is an example of woodwork on the very most basic human level.

"The important thing isn't the advertising of course, it is this notion that there are intrinsically human shapes and forms that address intrinsically human needs, matched with our material environment. There are things, objects that we have made and re-made, carried with us for thousands and thousands of years over continents and through cultures. Serving boards have to be among the earliest of all human tools.

"[A friend and I] once ended a very long and tiresome day of traveling and were greeted by our foreign hosts with a very beautiful and easy meal of charcuterie, toasts, fruits, and vegetables that was prepared on and served on a very large oak plank. There was no pretense about the meal, no waiting. The plank was able to move to the couches as we talked about our travels, then eventually outside in the evening under the stars. A movable feast. There were no dishes or portions served. There was no pressure. It was a communal meal."

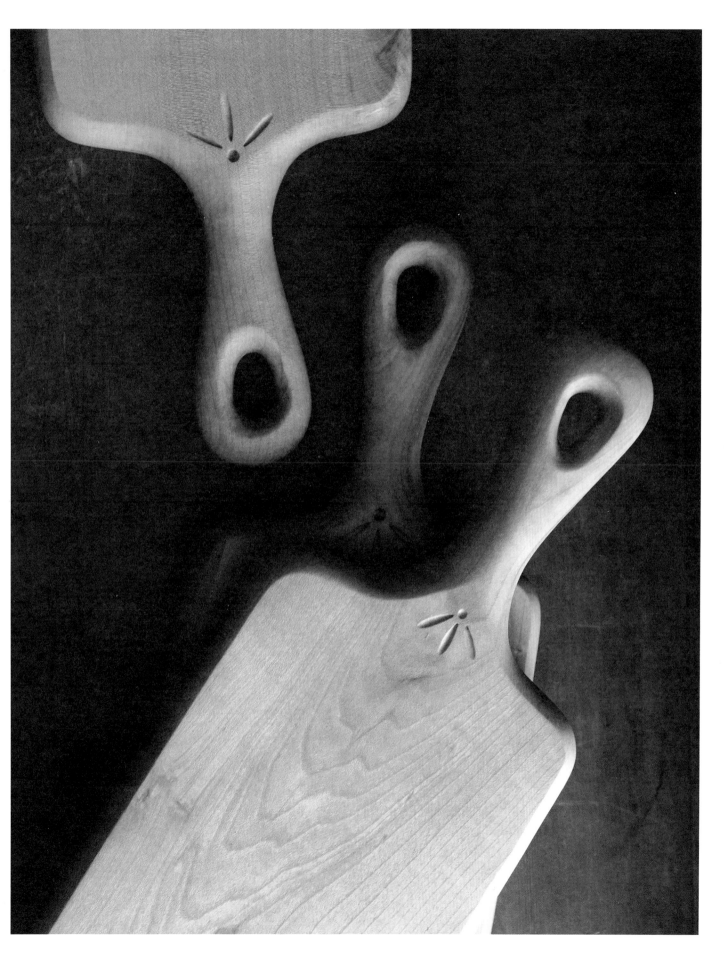

CHAPTER 1:

EXPERT ADVICE & INSIGHTS

While an empty serving board is bursting with potential, getting it to convey exactly what you want and satisfy your guests can be daunting. With that in mind, we begin with tips from culinary heavyweights like Murray's Cheese, Publican Quality Meats, Lady & Larder, and more, enabling you to get your board just right.

ELIZABETH CHUBBUCK'S PRIZE SERVING BOARD

❧

Elizabeth Chubbuck, Senior Vice President of Marketing & Sales for Murray's Cheese, picked her favorite cheeses for a board, along with some great tips for accompaniments.

❧

CHEESE

BARDEN BLUE: *A rich, buttery blue from Consider Bardwell Farm in West Pawlet, Vermont*

ANNELIES: *A sweet, raw cow's milk cheese that hails from Northern Switzerland. Famed cheese maker Walter Rass crafted this cheese as a tribute to his wife.*

STOCKINGHALL CHEDDAR: *Murray's own clothbound cheddar.*

GREENSWARD: *This washed-rind cow's milk cheese is the result of an exclusive collaboration between Murray's and Vermont's notorious Cellars at Jasper Hill*

HOLLANDER: *A taste that brings sweet cashews to mind makes this sheep's milk cheese from the Pyrenees a must-have*

SAINT-MAURE: *A standout goat cheese from a region that is famous for them: France's Loire Valley*

LAIT BLOOMER: *A flower-rinded Brie-style cheese from Jasper Hill Farm in Vermont*

FAVORITE ACCOMPANIMENTS

PRESERVED PUMPKIN: *An earthy preserve made from pumpkin, it goes well with a blue or alpine cheese*

CHERRY PRESERVES: *Cloves and tart cherries come together in this preserve, which is a perfect complement to Stilton or Brie*

CORNICHONS: *These tart, mildly sweet pickles are great on any board*

PEPPADEW PEPPERS: *A sweet pepper whose bright red color will add a little pop to your board*

JOE FRIETZE, PUBLICAN QUALITY MEATS

❧

Joe Frietze, Chef de Cuisine at Chicago's Publican Quality Meats,
creates the constantly changing menu at this neighborhood
butcher shop, café, and gourmet market. This is his Salami 101.

❧

When I was approached to contribute to this book I was a bit uncertain of what I could bring to the table (or the board). As a chef at Publican Quality Meats, I love eating charcuterie, and they make a wide variety of them to choose from. The menu includes salami, whole muscle, pâtés, and headcheeses. At Publican Quality Meats, we have a very meat-centric outlook on our charcuterie boards. Our method is to pair great meat, great bread, and simple garnishes so as not to take away from the 2 weeks to 2 years that some of our products need to reach the finished product. That being said, I think it best that we talk salami history to cover some of the basics of making these "magical" meats.

At a certain point in our evolution, human beings began to kill animals that were often much bigger than themselves in order to survive. This created a conundrum, as a lot of the time they had too much meat to eat before it all spoiled. What's a guy who just hunted down a bear to do?

As far back as 2200 BCE, humans realized they could slice meat really thin and let it hang in the sun, or salt it and let it dry. The Greeks were employing this salting method on hams as far back as 1500 BCE, while the Romans fed their soldiers fermented sausages due to the long-lasting quality of the meat.

It has only been in the past 100 years that society decided we should treat meat with these methods for flavor purposes, rather than just for preservation. Nowadays we can go to any grocery store and buy a solid, ready-to-eat salami to put on a sandwich or serve while entertaining guests.

Let's talk about a few basics of charcuterie making. I promise I won't get too detailed. Meats are generally about 75 percent water, which is one of the reasons why they spoil at a certain point. See, bacteria thrive with the help of moisture, oxygen, and temperature, which makes meat a prime target, no pun intended. By using salt, nitrates, good bacteria, temperature, moisture control, and time, we can control this reaction and create a properly dried finished product.

A TYPICAL SALAMI TIMELINE
AT PUBLICAN QUALITY MEATS

❧

1. *A freshly slaughtered pig shows up. We work predominantly with small Illinois farms, including Catalpa Groves, Slagel Family Farms, and several others. If I talk to a farmer on Sunday, he kills a pig on Monday, and I get it delivered to me on Wednesday. Our meat doesn't travel 3,000 miles in a bag from some person I've never met on a farm I've never been to. Plus, we only use meat from whole animals to make salami.*

2. *A charming, handsome butcher breaks down said pig. The shoulders are usually for sausage, the hams for salami or schnitzel, the bones for stock, and the skin for rinds. We then figure out how much and what flavor of salami it will become.*

3. *The meat is scaled to around 40 pounds a batch. Using an Excel formula, we calculate the ingredients needed to make a certain amount of a specific type of salami. For example, to make black pepper-flavored salami the formula would let us know we need a certain set amount of salt, pink salt, dextrose, garlic, wine, etc.*

4. *The meat is then cut into appropriate-sized pieces and marinated for 3 days. This marinating happens in the refrigerator and results in several complex changes to the meat. On the 3rd day we grind the meat, then place it into a larger mixer to partially emulsify it.*

5. *After its emulsified, the meat is stuffed into natural casing. We like beef middles because they are very consistent in size and shape. Next, we ferment.*

6. *Fermenting takes place at slightly higher than room temperature for approximately 48 hours. This fermentation allows bacteria to eat the sugars in our salami and convert them into lactic acid, which is what gives your salami its tangy flavor. Once we have achieved the proper pH level and have created an environment where the good bacteria can flourish, we start the aging process.*

7. *Publican Quality Meats has a digitally regulated moisture and temperature room that allows ambient bacteria in the air to flavor the salami as it ages and starts losing moisture content. Once the appropriate amount of moisture has been lost, we then have a product that is ready to be enjoyed. This usually takes about 6 to 8 weeks.*

❧

This process is significantly more complicated than this, but I think you get the gist of it. If you are interested in the science of it there are lots of great books on the production of salami. Whole muscle charcuterie follows a similar path. These include the coppas, bresolas, and lonzas of the world. These are a little harder to find outside of specialty shops but are fantastic if you can get your hands on them. Pâté, headcheese, and rillettes are cooked products that should always have a place on your board and can easily be made at home. Don't be scared to try new things—only eating prosciutto is really boring, sorry to tell you.

Now that you have some basic information, source some good products, cut it the right way, add some fun garnishes, and enjoy with friends. Or, if you're me, on your couch with your bare hands.

THE CHEESE STORE OF BEVERLY HILLS

❦

When Norbert Wabnig, owner of The Cheese Store of Beverly Hills, gathers with his wife, children, and grandchildren, there is often cheese involved. He handcrafts a cheese board with each and every one of his family members in mind. "Everyone has their own favorite," he says. "It's nice to have something on the board for everyone." Below are some of his favorites.

❦

ALPEN BLUMEN (ALPINE FLOWERS): COW'S MILK CHEESE FROM AUSTRIA
(It has lovely, dried meadow flowers in it.)

MOLITERNO: SHEEP'S MILK CHEESE MADE WITH A SMALL AMOUNT OF GOAT CHEESE
(Pairs well with truffles.)

ASHEN BLEU: COW'S MILK CHEESE
from Germany.

FROMAGER D' AFFINOIS: COW'S MILK CHEESE
similar to Brie, that comes from Rhône-Alpes.

SAINT ALBRAY: MADE FROM COW'S MILK
this cheese hails from Aquitaine in France.

LADY & LARDER

❧

Sarah Simms Hendrix, Matthew Simms, and Boo Simms are the sibling team behind Lady & Larder, a company that crafts artisan boards loaded with local ingredients. Combining artistic flair with the best local bounty, they create boards that are sought after all over Southern California. They are committed to small-batch producers and farmers, as well as American-made cheeses and cured meats. Their boards change from season to season, and in California that often means week to week. They stand by the claim that no two of their boards are ever the same.

Even if you can't find the exact ingredients that the professionals use, there are pairing dynamics to keep in mind when putting together a serving board. Here's how Lady & Larder thinks about composing one of its coveted serving boards.

❧

Always include one familiar cheese, like a cheddar, so that your guests immediately feel comfortable diving right in. After a glass of wine or two you will find that your guests tend to get a bit more adventurous.

❧

Texture. Texture. Texture. Use a variety of cheeses and make sure that your accoutrements include nuts, fruit, and olives to provide a mixture of salty and sweet flavors. Create variety by choosing cheeses from different categories, such as fresh, soft, semi-soft, hard, or blue.

❧

Another way of creating variety is by selecting your cheeses based on the type of milk they are made from. For a winning taste, don't hesitate to use cheeses made from the milk of cows, goats, and sheep.

Use local and seasonal accoutrements to create a sense of place and ensure deliciousness. In our boards, we use Malibu wild sage honey, assorted jams from INNA, and grainy mustard from Mustard & Co., as well as honeycomb, dried and fresh fruits, nuts, olives, and dates. For a festive touch, we make our own Sugar & Spiced Walnuts during the holiday season and fill the boards with lots of fresh Fuyu persimmons, Crimson Gold apples, pomegranates, figs, and winter citrus.

※

Work with odd numbers. For example, 3 cheeses and 2 different kinds of charcuterie equal 5 total options, which is most pleasing visually. Depending on the size of your group aim for 3, 5, or 7 options on your board, as well as seasonal accoutrements.

※

Cut or crumble hard cheeses so that they are more approachable to your guests. With softer cheeses, we prefer to leave them whole or halved for scooping and spreading. We love seeing the insides of softer cheeses, so we will often cut smaller wheels, like Mt. Tam, in half the way you would slice a bagel. That way guests can see the beautiful triple cream interior.

※

Always serve your cheese and cured meats at room temperature so that they can really shine!

※

The question we get asked most is how much you should serve on your board. You want to hit that sweet spot where you display enough cheese to allow for snacking but not ruin your guests' appetites if dinner is to follow. To ensure perfect portioning, plan on buying 3 to 4 oz. of cheese and charcuterie per guest.

A FAVORITE LADY & LARDER BOARD

❧

CYPRESS GROVE HUMBOLDT FOG

INNA HAYWARD KIWI JAM

POINT REYES BAY BLUE

FLYING DISC RANCH BARHI DATES

MT. TAM TRIPLE CREAM

MALIBU WILD SAGE HONEY

FAT UNCLE FARMS ALMONDS

LADY & LARDER'S FAVORITE VENDORS

❧

CHEESE	MEATS	ACCOUTREMENTS
Cowgirl Creamery	Elevation Meats & Charcuterie	Fat Uncle Farms
Cypress Grove	Red Table Meat Co.	Flying Disc Ranch
Jasper Hill Farm	La Quercia	Peacock Family Farm
Point Reyes Farmstead Cheese Co.	Salumi Artisan Cured Meats	Fillmore Farms
Central Coast Creamery	Charlito's Cocina	La Vigne Fruits
Bellwether Farms Creamery		Malibu Honey
Hook's Cheese Company Inc.		Mustard & Co.
Beecher's Handmade Cheese		

BLAKE HILL PRESERVES

❧

Vicky Allard and Joe Hanglin, founders of Blake Hill Preserves, are award-winning fine preserve makers located in Vermont. Vicky, a third-generation preserve maker, carries on her family's tradition by creating an inspired and creative line of products.

❧

"I am a third-generation English preserve maker, based in Vermont," Vicky said. "I grew up in the county of Hampshire in Southern England, foraging wild berries in the early morning with my father from hillsides and country lanes near our home, then returning to our kitchen to cook fresh jam with my mother and sister. We would be busy all summer long with our endeavors, so we could enjoy the flavor of fresh-picked summer fruits throughout the year.

"Many years later my husband and I moved to Vermont and purchased Blake Hill, an old farming property idyllically sited amongst the rolling hills surrounding Grafton, a quintessential small Vermont town. When we discovered wild blackberries growing at the edge of our woodlands near our farmhouse, fond memories of childhood foraging and jam making came flooding back and a weekend passion was rekindled with our first homemade jars of blackberry and apple jam.

"Shortly after a busy first summer of homemade jam making, a friend shared a few jars of our jam with the owner of Grafton's country store and we won our first order. After recovering from the surprise of an unexpected business launch, more local stores were keen to bring in our special line of foraged jams and chutneys and the business rapidly grew from there. We built our first dedicated Preserves Kitchen in the meadows at Blake Hill, and within three years of rapid growth built a much larger Preserves Kitchen at Artisans Park in Windsor, Vermont.

"Blake Hill now makes both sweet and savory preserves, marmalades, and spicy jams for some of the nation's leading cheese makers and mongers, including a special collection created in collaboration with our renowned cheese-making neighbors, Jasper Hill Farm. Our cheese pairing collection can be found in specialty cheese shops throughout the U.S., including Murray's Cheese in New York City, Di Bruno Bros. in Philadelphia, and, most recently, at The Better Cheddar in Kansas City, Missouri."

PERFECT PAIRINGS

❧

Vicky and Joe enjoy crafting bespoke fruit spreads for certain artisan cheeses. The following are three of their favorite preserves that have resulted from this process.

❧

SPICED PLUMS WITH PORT & ANISE

"One of our first preserves created for bespoke cheese pairings, this was created in partnership with Jasper Hill Farm for pairing with their eponymous Bayley Hazen. We wanted to create something that was almost fig-like with all the moistness and great acidity of some of the very best fall plums. This spiced jam has very little added sugar, allowing the natural sweetness of the heady balance of plums and sweet, rich prunes to shine. With a little apple cider vinegar, a dash of full-flavored tawny port, and a hint of anise that captures the notes of Bayley Hazen, this is a jam created in honor of one of our favorite varieties of blue."

WILD BLUEBERRY WITH THYME

"Winner of the 2018 U.S. Good Food Awards, this preserve was inspired by the abundance of wild thyme growing at Blake Hill and is phenomenal with a grassy goat cheese or Brie. It has the perfect balance of sweet and tart, a nice acidity which makes it great to pair with a creamy cheese. The subtle flavor of thyme pays homage to the grassy notes of our favorite goat cheese from Vermont Creamery."

RASPBERRY WITH WILD BERGAMOT

"Part of our special edition line of Vermont Forager jams, this is delicious with soft creamy cheese such as Jasper Hill's Harbison, Vermont Creamery's Cremont, and Vermont Farmstead's Lille. We harvest wild bergamot flowers from our gardens at Blake Hill, infuse them for 48 hours to make an aromatic, lightly peppery wild bergamot tea, and then combine this with fresh local raspberries to make the most deliciously floral, sweet yet slightly tart, spiced raspberry-wild bergamot jam that lusciously embraces some of our favorite creamy cheeses."

ESTERS WINE SHOP & BAR
SANTA MONICA, CA

❧

*Kathryn Coker started working as a server right out of college
and fell in love with the restaurant life. That relationship led to the
discovery of her true love: wine. "The stories behind the bottles are
what really hooked me on this life-long passion," she said.*

*After moving from New York to Los Angeles, she got a job at Rustic
Canyon Wine Bar and Seasonal Kitchen, where she worked her way through
the ranks and eventually became the restaurant's wine director. While
working together, Coker and CEO Josh Loeb came up with the idea for Esters,
a wine bar that would also be a retail shop; two years later they opened.*

*Executive Chef Jessica Liu works closely with Coker to create
new and interesting items for the cheese boards at Esters, which are
ever changing and often surprising. Coker maintains that the key to
a serving board is including whatever food gets you excited.*

Below are some of her other recommendations.

❧

I love cheeses and meats from boutique producers, local if possible.

❧

Accompaniments should also be really special. We are just a few blocks
from the Santa Monica Farmers Market. Our chef makes a seasonal fruit
mostarda that's always fabulous: tangy and not too sweet.

❧

I also love the pepper jam that one of our servers' mother makes. She grows the peppers in her backyard and makes this jam in bulk just for Esters. It's truly something special that guests come back for time and again. It's sweet, spicy, and perfect with gooey, salty cheese.

❧

Pair cheese with nuts, mostarda, compote, or honey.

❧

With meat, I just love cornichons. There can never be enough cornichons.

Coker also shared some Champagnes that will go well with any serving board.

❧

EXTRA BRUT,
PLOYEZ-JACQUEMART, FRANCE 2005

Crazy delicious value for vintage Champagne.

❧

1ER CRU BRUT, "CACHET D'OR," J. LASSALLE,
MONTAGNE DE REIMS, FRANCE NV

*A classic and total crowd-pleaser! Three generations
of women have run this fantastic estate.*

❧

BRUT, "LES SEPT CRUS," AGRAPART,
CÔTE DES BLANCS, AVIZE, FRANCE NV

*Always the somm's choice, an original grower and
producer in Champagne who never disappoints!*

❧

GRAND CRU, 'BRUT INITIALE',
JACQUES SELOSSE, AVIZE, CRAMANT,
AND OGER, FRANCE NV

The ultimate splurge from a profound winemaker producing terrior-driven bubbles.

❧

GRAND CRU, BRUT ROSÉ,
CAMILLE SAVÉS, BOUZY, FRANCE NV

Pure elegance, the best rosé Champagne from the most dapper man in Bouzy.

STOVETOPPED FINE FOODS

❧

*Lisa Walker is a classically trained Northern California chef.
She owns the Los Angeles-based special event planning firm Stovetopped
Fine Foods with Edward Vicedo. She has cooked for a wide range of
clientele, from celebrities and titans of finance to local, state, and world
leaders. Below, she outlines her philosophy when building a board.*

❧

"A live cut wooden board emotes all things natural and says two things: first, that we appreciate nature and beauty; secondly, this food is all-natural," Walker said. "The very nature of the board demands seasonal ingredients. In the colder months, we like to bake an apple filled with sage and sausage and pair with goat cheese and toasted bread for a beautiful presentation. A chilled sparkling wine or cider with refreshing notes of fruit and effervescence make excellent pairings with our favorite serving board. When we prepare our boards, local, seasonal, and traditional is what comes readily to mind."

STOVETOPPED FINE FOODS FAVORITE SEASONAL BOARD PAIRINGS

❧

Spring & Summer

FRESH SEASONAL FRUIT AND VEGETABLES

AIOLI, MUSTARDS,
TAPENADES, CAPERS, PICKLES

GRILLED SEASONAL VEGETABLES

GRILLED MEATS AND FISH, SUCH AS CEDAR
PLANK FISH, PORTERHOUSE STEAK, BEEF
TENDERLOIN, AND CHICKEN UNDER A BRICK

❧

Fall & Winter

ROASTED MEATS SUCH AS PORK LOIN, TURKEY
BREASTS, FILET MIGNON, DUCK, PHEASANT,
SAUSAGES, PORK BELLY, AND BACON

BAKED AND TOASTED SEASONAL VEGETABLES

WARM CHICORY, KALE, AND SPINACH SALADS

MUSTARDS, PICKLES, MOSTARDA,
JAMS, AND COMPOTES

CURED MEATS

CURED FISH

SMOKED FISH

SALAD GREENS

MIKE'S HOT HONEY

❧

The inspiration for Mike's Hot Honey came to Mike Kurtz while he was traveling through Brazil and was introduced to chili infused honey. He came back to the states and began experimenting with a variety of chili peppers and local honey to make his own version of the spicy honey. Here are some of this favorite pairings.

❧

FRESH RICOTTA

GOAT CHEESE

MANCHEGO

BLUE CHEESE

SHARP CHEDDAR

BRIE

GORGONZOLA

SOPPRESSATA

PROSCIUTTO

SPECK

CANDIED NUTS

FIGS

BOSC PEARS

GRANNY SMITH APPLES

CHAPTER 2:

CRACKERS & BREADS

One of the many appealing aspects of centering parties and meals around serving boards is that many little bites can be had. Perhaps you fill up a plate with whatever's on offer, or perhaps you pick and choose as the spirit strikes, a cube of cheese here, a slice of meat there. But as you will see, serving boards are about much more than meat and cheese, and the recipes that follow provide a wide range of textures and flavor profiles that will enhance whatever you decide to populate your board with.

Sea Salt and Herb Crackers

YIELD: **12 CRACKERS**

ACTIVE TIME: **10 MINUTES**

TOTAL TIME: **1 HOUR AND 15 MINUTES**

These light crackers will add just enough flavor to enhance whatever you choose to top them with.

INGREDIENTS

2 CUPS ALL-PURPOSE FLOUR

1 ½ TEASPOONS
 BAKING POWDER

1 CUP WATER

3 TABLESPOONS OLIVE
 OIL, PLUS MORE FOR
 BRUSHING

1 TEASPOON FINE SEA SALT

1 TEASPOON PAPRIKA

1 TEASPOON BLACK PEPPER

FLAKY SEA SALT, TO TASTE

FRESH HERBS,
 FINELY CHOPPED

DIRECTIONS

1. Preheat oven to 425°F.

2. Mix the flour, baking powder, water, olive oil, fine sea salt, paprika, and pepper in a small bowl. Let rest in the refrigerator for an hour.

3. Line a baking sheet with parchment.

4. Form the dough into small balls and roll them out into long, paper-thin rectangles.

5. Place the crackers on a baking sheet and brush generously with olive oil. Sprinkle with flaky sea salt and fresh herbs.

6. Bake for 5 minutes, or until the crackers are golden brown. Let cool on a wire rack before serving.

Rosemary Crackers

YIELD: **6 CRACKERS**

ACTIVE TIME: **15 MINUTES**

TOTAL TIME: **1 HOUR AND 10 MINUTES**

If you're thinking of loading your board up with meat, you should take advantage of the sharp flavor provided by these crackers.

INGREDIENTS

⅛ TEASPOON DRIED YEAST

1 TABLESPOON WARM WATER

¾ CUP ALL-PURPOSE FLOUR

½ TEASPOON SALT

PINCH OF SUGAR

1 TABLESPOON ROSEMARY, LEAVES REMOVED AND CHOPPED

DIRECTIONS

1. Preheat oven to 350°F.

2. Place the yeast and the warm water in a bowl and let stand for 10 minutes.

3. Add the remaining ingredients to the bowl and knead until a smooth dough forms.

4. Cover and let stand in a warm spot for 15 to 20 minutes, or until the dough doubles in size.

5. On a lightly floured surface, roll out the dough as thin as you can without tearing it.

6. Cut crackers to desired shape and place on a parchment-lined baking sheet. Brush the crackers with a small amount of olive oil.

7. Place in oven and bake for 20 minutes, or until golden brown. Let cool on a wire rack before serving.

Purple Potato Chips

YIELD: **4 TO 6 SERVINGS**

ACTIVE TIME: **5 MINUTES**

TOTAL TIME: **20 MINUTES**

Purple potato chips add a completely unique presentation aspect to your board and go well with any dip.

INGREDIENTS

3 LARGE PURPLE POTATOES

4 TABLESPOONS OLIVE OIL

2 TEASPOONS SEA SALT

DIRECTIONS

1. Preheat oven to 400°F.

2. Thinly slice the potatoes. Use a mandoline if you want them extremely thin, or to create ruffled edges.

3. Place the potatoes and the olive oil in a bowl and toss until the potatoes are evenly coated. Place the potatoes on a baking sheet in a single layer. Bake for 12 to 15 minutes, or until crispy.

4. Remove from the oven, transfer to a bowl, add the salt, and toss lightly. Serve warm or store in an airtight container.

Beet Chips

These bloodred roots make beautiful and delicious crisps.

YIELD: **4 TO 6 SERVINGS**

ACTIVE TIME: **5 MINUTES**

TOTAL TIME: **20 MINUTES**

INGREDIENTS

5 FRESH BEETS, PEELED

4 TABLESPOONS OLIVE OIL

2 TEASPOONS SEA SALT

DIRECTIONS

1. Preheat the oven to 400°F.

2. Thinly slice the beets. Place the beets and the olive oil in a bowl and toss until the slices are evenly coated. Place on a baking sheet in a single layer. Bake for 12 to 15 minutes, or until golden brown.

3. Remove from the oven, transfer to a bowl, add the salt, and toss. Serve warm or store in an airtight container.

Rye Crackers

The earthy, spicy flavor of rye makes these crackers a welcome addition to any board.

YIELD: **12 CRACKERS**

ACTIVE TIME: **10 MINUTES**

TOTAL TIME: **30 MINUTES**

INGREDIENTS

2 CUPS RYE FLOUR

2 TEASPOONS SALT

FRESHLY GROUND BLACK PEPPER, TO TASTE

1 CUP OLIVE OIL

2 CUPS WATER

2 TABLESPOONS SESAME AND/OR SUNFLOWER SEEDS (OPTIONAL)

DIRECTIONS

1. Preheat the oven to 350°F.

2. Mix all ingredients other than the seeds in a bowl. Place the dough on a flour-dusted surface and roll it out until approximately ¼-inch thick. Use cookie cutters to shape the crackers and, if desired, sprinkle with sesame and/or sunflower seeds. You can also use a fork to punch some small holes in the crackers, but this is optional.

3. Place the crackers on a parchment-lined baking sheet for 20 minutes. Let cool on a wire rack before serving.

Parmesan Crisps

YIELD: 8 CRISPS

ACTIVE TIME: 10 MINUTES

TOTAL TIME: 10 MINUTES

These simple, lacy crisps are quick and can be made well in advance. They are best stored in an airtight container.

INGREDIENTS

½ CUP PARMESAN CHEESE, GRATED

DIRECTIONS

1. Preheat oven to 400°F.

2. Pour a tablespoon of Parmesan onto a parchment-lined baking sheet and lightly pat down. Repeat with the remaining cheese, spacing each spoonful about a ½ inch apart.

3. Bake for 3 to 5 minutes, or until golden and crisp. Let cool on a wire rack before serving.

Crispy Wonton Skins

YIELD: 4 TO 6 SERVINGS

ACTIVE TIME: 5 MINUTES

TOTAL TIME: 10 MINUTES

Made from simple wonton wrappers, these crispy "skins" go especially well with Asian-inspired dips.

INGREDIENTS

2 CUPS VEGETABLE OIL

4 WONTON WRAPPERS, CUT INTO TRIANGLES

SALT, TO TASTE

DIRECTIONS

1. Place the oil in a Dutch oven and cook over medium-high heat until it is 300°F.

2. Place the wonton wrappers in the Dutch oven and turn frequently until crispy and golden brown.

3. Use a slotted spoon to remove the fried wonton wrappers from the oil and set on paper towels to drain.

4. Season with salt and serve.

Prosciutto Chips

Charcuterie and chips combined, these are an elegant addition to any spread.

YIELD: **4 TO 6 SERVINGS**

ACTIVE TIME: **3 MINUTES**

TOTAL TIME: **15 TO 18 MINUTES**

INGREDIENTS

20 SLICES OF PROSCIUTTO, SLICED THIN

DIRECTIONS

1. Preheat oven to 400°F. Lay slices of prosciutto flat on a baking sheet. Don't worry about placing the slices too close together as they will shrink as they cook.

2. Place baking sheet in the oven and bake for 12 to 15 minutes, or until the prosciutto is crispy. Serve warm.

Caraway Water Biscuits

Biscuits that are light and airy enough to elevate any occasion.

YIELD: **4 TO 6 SERVINGS**

ACTIVE TIME: **5 MINUTES**

TOTAL TIME: **15 MINUTES**

INGREDIENTS

⅛ CUP ALL-PURPOSE FLOUR

10 TABLESPOONS WATER

⅛ TEASPOON SALT

2 TABLESPOONS CARAWAY SEEDS

DIRECTIONS

1. Preheat oven to 350°F.

2. Add the flour and water to a mixing bowl and whisk until combined. Add the salt.

3. On a parchment-lined baking sheet, use a pastry brush to transfer the batter to the sheet, taking care to make nice, long crackers.

4. Sprinkle with caraway seeds and place in the oven. Bake for 8 minutes, or until golden brown. Remove the sheet and let the crackers cool before serving.

Cheese Twists

YIELD: **12 TO 15 SERVINGS**

ACTIVE TIME: **15 TO 20 MINUTES**

TOTAL TIME: **30 MINUTES**

Feel free to try other combinations of cheeses to create different-tasting twists.

INGREDIENTS

2 PUFF PASTRY SHEETS, THAWED

½ CUP FONTINA CHEESE, GRATED

½ CUP PARMESAN CHEESE, GRATED

1 TEASPOON FRESH
    THYME, MINCED

1 TEASPOON FRESHLY
    GROUND BLACK PEPPER

1 EGG, BEATEN

DIRECTIONS

1. Preheat oven to 375°F.

2. Roll out puff pastry until the sheets are approximately 10 by 12 inches.

3. In a bowl, combine the cheeses, thyme, and pepper.

4. Lightly brush the tops of the pastry sheets with the egg. Then, sprinkle the cheese mixture over the pastry sheets and lightly press down so the mixture sticks to the surface.

5. Cut the sheets into ¼-inch thick strips and twist. Then, place twists on a baking sheet. Bake for 12 to 15 minutes, or until twists are golden brown and puffy. Turn over each twist to ensure even browning and allow to cook for an additional 2 to 3 minutes.

6. Remove twists from the oven and let cool on a wire rack before serving.

Pretzels

YIELD: **8 PRETZELS**

ACTIVE TIME: **20 MINUTES**

TOTAL TIME: **1 HOUR AND 20 MINUTES**

Pair these pretzels with your favorite ale and horseradish or mustard.

INGREDIENTS

2 ¼ TEASPOONS INSTANT YEAST

1 CUP WATER AT 110ºF

1 TEASPOON SUGAR

2 ½ CUPS ALL-PURPOSE FLOUR

½ TEASPOON SEA SALT

½ CUP WARM WATER

1 TABLESPOON BAKING SODA

VEGETABLE OIL FOR GREASING THE BAKING SHEET

COARSE SEA SALT, FOR TOPPING

3 TABLESPOONS UNSALTED BUTTER, MELTED

DIRECTIONS

1. Preheat oven to 450°F.

2. Combine the yeast, 110°F water, and sugar in a small bowl and let sit for 10 minutes until frothy. Add the flour and salt. Mix by hand for a few seconds to roughly combine, then knead. The dough should feel soft and smooth.

3. Cover and let rise for 30 minutes.

4. Grease a baking sheet with vegetable oil.

5. Place the dough onto a lightly oiled countertop and cut it into eight pieces.

6. Combine the warm water and baking soda and microwave for 1 minute.

7. Roll each of the eight pieces into a long rope, then shape into pretzels. Dip each pretzel into the baking soda-and-water mixture then transfer to the greased baking sheet. Sprinkle with the coarse sea salt and let rest for 10 minutes.

8. Bake for 9 to 10 minutes until the pretzels are golden brown. Once out of the oven, brush the pretzels with the melted butter while they are still hot.

RUSTIC BAKERY

RUSTIC BAKERY, NOW A MAINSTAY IN MARIN COUNTY, California, was founded by Carol LeValley and her husband Josh Harris. A trip to the famous Cowgirl Creamery in Point Reyes Station, California, inspired LeValley to turn her passion for baking into a business, as the creamery's cheeses set dreams of a perfect flatbread cracker dancing in her head. She got to work immediately and used a carefully curated presentation to secure an order of 50 cases per week from the creamery.

LeValley and her husband now have four cafés, a growing wholesale business, and clients as varied as Pope Francis, George Lucas, and Virgin Airlines. Although LeValley won't give out the top-secret recipe for the coveted flatbread cracker, she did share a few of her favorites, including the Feta and Herb Quickbread on the next page. As you might expect, each one would be a great addition to any serving board.

Rustic Bakery Feta and Herb Quickbread

YIELD: **1 LOAF**

ACTIVE TIME: **10 MINUTES**

TOTAL TIME: **1 HOUR**

One of Rustic Bakery's most popular recipes, Carol adapted this recipe from Clotilde Dusoulier, the blogger behind Chocolate & Zucchini. This savory bread pairs well with fresh vegetables and sweet spreads.

INGREDIENTS

1 PAT UNSALTED BUTTER

2 TABLESPOONS SESAME SEEDS

150 GRAMS (1 ¼ CUPS)
    ALL-PURPOSE FLOUR

1 TABLESPOON BAKING POWDER

3 LARGE ORGANIC EGGS

¼ CUP OLIVE OIL

½ CUP PLAIN UNSWEETENED
    YOGURT, PLUS 2 TABLESPOONS

½ TEASPOON FINE SEA SALT

½ TEASPOON FRESHLY
    GROUND PEPPER

7 OZ. SHEEP OR GOAT'S
    MILK FETA CHEESE

1 CUP OF FRESH HERB LEAVES,
    CHOPPED (MIXTURE OF ITALIAN
    PARSLEY, BASIL, CHERVIL,
    CHIVES, AND MINT)

DIRECTIONS

1. Preheat the oven to 350°F. Butter a 9-by-5-inch loaf pan and sprinkle half of the sesame seeds onto the bottom and sides, shaking the pan to coat.

2. Combine the flour and baking powder in a bowl. In a separate bowl, whisk together the eggs, oil, yogurt, salt, and pepper. Stir in the cheese and herbs.

3. Fold the flour mixture into the egg mixture. Be careful not to overmix the batter, it is okay if a few lumps remain.

4. Pour the batter into the prepared pan. Level the surface with a spatula and sprinkle the remaining sesame seeds on top.

5. Bake for 40 to 50 minutes until the top is golden and a knife inserted in the center comes out clean.

6. Allow to cool for a few minutes and run a knife around the pan to loosen. Unmold and transfer to a rack to cool. Cut into slices or cubes. Serve slightly warm or at room temperature.

Dense Fruit Bread

YIELD: **1 LOAF**

ACTIVE TIME: **25 MINUTES**

TOTAL TIME: **1 HOUR AND 30 MINUTES**

Tweaking a recipe from the well-known blog **Not Quite Nigella** *resulted in this decadent bread.*

INGREDIENTS

5 OZ. PRUNES

5 OZ. DRIED CRANBERRIES

5 OZ. PITTED DATES

5 OZ. GOLDEN RAISINS

3 CUPS APPLE CIDER

1 TEASPOON BAKING SODA

½ CUP BROWN SUGAR

2 CUPS ALL-PURPOSE FLOUR

2 TEASPOONS GROUND CINNAMON

1 TEASPOON GROUND GINGER

2 EGGS

DIRECTIONS

1. Preheat oven to 350°F and line a standard loaf pan with parchment paper.

2. Place fruit and 2 cups of apple cider in a saucepan and bring to a simmer. Allow to simmer for 20 minutes or until the fruit has absorbed the liquid. Stir in baking soda and set aside.

3. Add the brown sugar, flour, cinnamon, and ginger to a small bowl and stir until well combined. Stir in the eggs. Then, add the fruit mixture and the remaining apple cider. Stir until well combined and pour into prepared loaf pan.

4. Bake for 45 minutes or until an inserted skewer comes out clean. Remove from the oven and let cool for a few minutes. Run a knife around the pan to loosen, then unmold and transfer to a wire rack to cool.

New England Brown Bread

This sweet bread can be served with anything pungent or salty. Slices of grilled sausages and spicy mustard are also good partners.

YIELD: **1 LOAF**

ACTIVE TIME: **15 MINUTES**

TOTAL TIME: **1 HOUR**

INGREDIENTS

BUTTER FOR GREASING COFFEE CAN OR LOAF PAN

½ CUP ALL-PURPOSE FLOUR

½ CUP RYE FLOUR

½ CUP FINELY GROUND CORNMEAL

½ TEASPOON BAKING POWDER

½ TEASPOON BAKING SODA

½ TEASPOON SALT

½ TEASPOON NUTMEG

1 CUP BUTTERMILK

½ CUP MOLASSES

DIRECTIONS

1. Preheat oven to 325°F.

2. Bring a pot of water to a boil.

3. Grease a standard coffee can or a small loaf pan with the butter.

4. In a large bowl, mix together the all-purpose flour, rye flour, cornmeal, baking powder, baking soda, salt, and nutmeg.

5. In another bowl, whisk together the buttermilk and molasses.

6. Combine the wet and dry ingredients and stir well with a spoon. Pour batter into can or pan, making sure to only fill about two-thirds of the way.

7. Cover the loaf pan or coffee can tightly with foil and place it into a baking pan.

8. Pour the boiling water into the baking pan until it reaches one-third up the side of the coffee can or loaf pan. Put the baking pan into the oven.

9. Bake for 45 minutes or until a toothpick inserted into the middle comes out clean. Let cool slightly before serving.

Classic Stout Bread

YIELD: **2 LOAVES**

ACTIVE TIME: **10 MINUTES**

TOTAL TIME: **1 HOUR AND 10 MINUTES**

This recipe comes via my grandmother, who used to serve it with slices of sharp cheddar.

INGREDIENTS

2 ¼ CUPS WHOLE WHEAT FLOUR

1 CUP ROLLED OATS, PLUS
    MORE FOR TOPPING

½ CUP BROWN SUGAR

2 ¼ TEASPOONS BAKING SODA

1 TEASPOON BAKING POWDER

½ TEASPOON SALT

⅓ CUP BUTTER, MELTED

1 CUP BUTTERMILK

1 BOTTLE OF GUINNESS
    OR OTHER STOUT

DIRECTIONS

1. Preheat oven to 400°F and grease 2 loaf pans.

2. Stir dry ingredients in a bowl and set aside. In a separate bowl, combine the butter, buttermilk, and beer.

3. Place the wet and dry ingredients together and stir until well combined. Pour into prepared loaf pans and sprinkle with additional oats.

4. Bake for 1 hour or until a knife inserted into the middle of the loaves comes out clean. Let cool on a wire rack before serving.

Classic Pita Bread

YIELD: **16 PITAS**

ACTIVE TIME: **60 MINUTES**

TOTAL TIME: **2 HOURS**

And here's an easy recipe for another flatbread that originated in the Mediterranean region, purportedly ancient Greece, as the word itself is Greek—pektos— meaning solid or clotted. It is popular around the world.

INGREDIENTS

1 PACKET ACTIVE DRY YEAST
(2 ¼ TEASPOONS)

2 ½ CUPS WATER (110–115°F)

3 CUPS FLOUR

1 TABLESPOON OLIVE OIL

1 TABLESPOON SALT

3 CUPS WHOLE WHEAT FLOUR

DIRECTIONS

1. Proof the yeast by mixing with the warm water. Let sit for about 10 minutes until foamy.

2. In a large bowl, add the yeast mix into the regular flour and stir until it forms a stiff dough. Cover and let the dough rise for about 1 hour.

3. Add the oil and salt to the dough and stir in the whole wheat flour in half-cup increments. When finished, the dough should be soft. Turn onto a lightly floured surface and knead it until it is smooth and elastic, about 10 minutes.

4. Coat the bottom and sides of a large mixing bowl (ceramic is best) with butter. Place the ball of dough in the bowl, cover loosely with plastic wrap, put it in a naturally warm, draft-free location, and let it rise until doubled in size, about 45 minutes to 1 hour.

5. On a lightly floured surface, punch down the dough and cut into 16 pieces. Put the pieces on a baking sheet and cover with a dish towel while working with individual pieces.

6. Roll out the pieces with a rolling pin until they are approximately 7 inches across. Stack them between sheets of plastic wrap.

7. Heat the skillet over high heat and lightly oil the bottom.Cook the individual pitas about 20 seconds on one side, then flip and cook for about a minute on the other side, until bubbles form. Turn again and continue to cook until the pita puffs up, another minute or so. Keep the skillet lightly oiled while processing, and store the pitas on a plate under a clean dish towel until ready to serve.

Quick Baguette

YIELD: **2 LOAVES**

ACTIVE TIME: **10 MINUTES**

TOTAL TIME: **2 HOURS**

Adapted from Mark Bittman, this simple baguette can be the star on any board, especially when people find out you made it yourself.

INGREDIENTS

2 ¼ TEASPOONS ACTIVE DRY YEAST

1 CUP LUKEWARM WATER

3 ½ CUPS ALL-PURPOSE FLOUR

2 TEASPOONS SALT

DIRECTIONS

1. Preheat oven to 400°F.

2. In a large bowl, mix yeast into the water and let sit 5 minutes. Add 3 cups of the flour and the salt. Mix until combined.

3. Knead until dough is smooth and elastic. Shape dough into a ball and place in a lightly greased bowl. Cover with plastic wrap and let rise until doubled in size, about 1 hour.

4. Punch down the dough and divide it into two pieces. Roll each piece into a foot-long loaf.

5. Place the loaves side by side, about 3 to 4 inches apart, on a baking sheet lined with floured parchment paper.

6. Cover with plastic wrap. Let the loaves rise for about 30 minutes and remove plastic wrap. Using a sharp knife, score the top of each loaf, making diagonal slits that are approximately ½-inch deep.

7. Place baguettes in oven. Reduce heat to 375°F and bake until golden brown, about 20 to 25 minutes. The inside of the bread should read close to 210°F on a thermometer when it is done.

8. Remove from the oven and spritz with water.

CHAPTER 3:

CHEESE

While the dizzying styles and varieties of cheese can be intimidating, there is no shortage of fine cheese makers and world-class cheese mongers whose expertise will help you identify which selections and preparations will be right for your serving board.

MURRAY'S CHEESE

AN IMPORTANT PART OF NEW YORK CITY'S culinary history, Murray's Cheese was founded in 1940 by Murray Greenberg, a Jewish veteran of the Spanish Civil War. In the '70s he sold the shop to his clerk, Louis Tudda, an immigrant from Calabria, Italy. The shop catered to the Greenwich Village neighborhood, carrying simple provisions like butter, eggs, and some cheeses. Fueled by his passion for cheese, Rob Kaufelt bought the shop in 1991 and started to travel all over the world, searching for products that would enable him to turn the shop into a destination for specialty cheeses and fine foods.

Kaufelt's vision never wavered, and today Murray's Cheese has two locations in New York City, over 600 restaurant and hotel clients, year-round educational programs, an e-commerce business, and a thriving restaurant.

Elizabeth Chubbuck, who provided us some of her favorite cheeses and accompaniments on page 8, has watched the company evolve into the shop it is today. "We have become much more than just a destination for the best cheeses in the world. We have become a teaching center, sharing our expertise and knowledge about cheese," she explains. "As the interest in food has grown, so has the interest in cheese."

The classic cheese board is a constant focus at Murray's because they have such an extensive selection of quality products. "For us," says Chubbuck, "it is about providing the knowledge and the ever-changing product line to create a cheese board that truly inspires."

Murray's Cheese Baked Brie Two Ways

YIELD: **4 TO 6 SERVINGS**

ACTIVE TIME: **10 MINUTES**

TOTAL TIME: **25 MINUTES**

A note on all Murray's Cheese recipes: Murray's produces several of its own cheeses and cured meats; these recipes have been adapted since not everyone can get Murray's products. But if you have access to them we wholly endorse using them!

INGREDIENTS

8 OZ. BRIE OR CAMEMBERT

1 BAGUETTE, SLICED

FOR SAVORY TOPPING:

¼ CUP ROASTED TOMATOES, CHOPPED

¼ CUP ARTICHOKES, CHOPPED

2 TABLESPOONS PITTED OLIVES, CHOPPED

1 TABLESPOON CAPERS

PINCH OF BLACK PEPPER

FOR SWEET TOPPING:

¼ CUP PECANS, CHOPPED

¼ CUP DRIED APRICOTS, CHOPPED

⅓ CUP DIVINA FIG SPREAD

¼ CUP DRIED CHERRIES

PINCH OF GROUND CINNAMON

DIRECTIONS

1. Preheat oven to 350°F.

2. Place your cheese in a ceramic Brie baker and top it with your mixture of choice.

3. Bake for 15 minutes, or until cheese is gooey.

4. Remove from oven. Serve with slices of baguette, which are intended to be dipped directly into the cheese.

The Big Dipper: Murray's Cheese Classic Fondue

YIELD: **6 SERVINGS**

ACTIVE TIME: **10 MINUTES**

TOTAL TIME: **20 MINUTES**

Some recommendations to serve along with this delicious fondue are: cornichons, Genoa salami, Rick's Picks Smokra, Calabrese salami, crusty bread, Rick's Picks People's Pickle, cipollini onions, and soppressata.

INGREDIENTS

1 POUND CAVE-AGED GRUYÈRE, SHREDDED

½ POUND EMMENTALER, SHREDDED

½ POUND GOUDA, SHREDDED

2 TABLESPOONS CORNSTARCH

1 GARLIC CLOVE

1 CUP WHITE WINE

1 TABLESPOON LEMON JUICE

SALT, PEPPER, AND GRATED NUTMEG, TO TASTE

DIRECTIONS

1. In a bowl, toss the shredded cheeses with the cornstarch until the cheese is well-coated.

2. Cut the garlic clove in half. Rub the inside of a crock-pot or fondue pot with garlic, then add the wine and lemon juice and bring to a simmer over low heat.

3. Add the cheese mixture all at once. Using a wooden spoon, stir over medium-low heat until the cheese is melted and smooth, about 5 to 10 minutes.

4. Season with salt, pepper, and grated nutmeg.

5. Dip your favorite accompaniments into the fondue and enjoy with friends.

FONDUE FOLKLORE: One of the most popular fondue customs is if a lady loses her bread cube in the fondue, she owes the man to her right a kiss. If a man has a similar mishap when dining in a restaurant, he should buy the next round of drinks. At home, he owes his hostess a kiss. Another fun fondue tradition is to leave a thin layer of fondue at the bottom of the caquelon (fondue pot). By carefully controlling the heat, you can form this layer into a crust known as "La Religieuse": The Religious One. Lift it out and distribute it among your guests. You'll see why it is considered a delicacy.

Murray's Cheese Beer Cheese

YIELD: **8 SERVINGS**

ACTIVE TIME: **5 MINUTES**

TOTAL TIME: **60 MINUTES**

Almost any bread or cracker will go well with this cheese, but pretzel rolls are what those in the know go with.

INGREDIENTS

1 POUND CHEDDAR, GRATED

4 OZ. CREAM CHEESE, AT ROOM TEMPERATURE

1 GARLIC CLOVE, FINELY GRATED

¼ CUP RED WINE

1 TABLESPOON WHOLE GRAIN MUSTARD

1 TEASPOON DIJON MUSTARD

2 TEASPOONS WORCESTERSHIRE SAUCE

½ TEASPOON PAPRIKA

1 CUP BLACK HOG GRANOLA BROWN ALE OR OTHER BROWN ALE AT ROOM TEMPERATURE

DIRECTIONS

1. Put all of the ingredients in a food processor, except for the beer, and puree until well combined.

2. Pour in ½ cup of the beer and continue to blend. Slowly add the rest of the beer a bit at a time, blending between each addition.

3. Cover and refrigerate for 1 hour before serving.

4. If using, toast the pretzel rolls in the oven until warmed through.

Murray's Cheese Raclette at Home

YIELD: **4 SERVINGS**

ACTIVE TIME: **10 MINUTES**

TOTAL TIME: **15 MINUTES**

This spread is so impressive that you just might hesitate to let people know how easy it is to throw together.

INGREDIENTS

1 POUND FRENCH RACLETTE

3 OZ. PROSCIUTTO DI PARMA

3 OZ. SPECK (ITALIAN CURED HAM)

3 OZ. CHORIZO

3 OZ. CORNICHONS

OLIVES

SMALL POTATOES, BOILED

BRUSSEL SPROUTS, ROASTED

BUTTERNUT SQUASH, ROASTED

CIPOLLINI ONIONS

CAULIFLOWER

ARTISANAL BREAD

PICKLED JALAPEÑO PEPPERS

FRUITS FOR DIPPING (SUCH AS SLICED APPLES AND PEARS)

FRUITS FOR REFRESHING THE PALATE (SUCH AS GRAPES, BERRIES AND DRIED FRUITS)

DIRECTIONS

1. Compose a board from the selection of breads, meats, fruits, and vegetables.

2. To heat the Raclette, use a raclette machine, skillet, or small baking dish. Slice the Raclette, place it in your vessel of choice, and heat it until the cheese is bubbly and gooey.

3. Pour the melted cheese over the personalized board and enjoy immediately.

Rustic Bakery Fromage Blanc with Herbs

YIELD: **4 TO 6 SERVINGS**

ACTIVE TIME: **1 MINUTE**

TOTAL TIME: **1 MINUTE**

Another winner courtesy of Anne LeValley. This French classic is traditionally served as a starter, but I like it as a dip or spread.

INGREDIENTS

4 OZ. FROMAGE BLANC

ZEST OF 6 LEMONS

4 TABLESPOONS LEMON JUICE

3 TABLESPOONS PARSLEY, MINCED

3 TABLESPOONS MINT, MINCED

3 TABLESPOONS DILL, MINCED

SALT AND PEPPER, TO TASTE

DIRECTIONS

1. Combine all ingredients in the bowl of a 5-quart mixer. Mix with paddle attachment until well combined.

Cheese Store of Beverly Hills Cheese Fondue

YIELD: **4 SERVINGS**

ACTIVE TIME: **10 MINUTES**

TOTAL TIME: **15 MINUTES**

According to Norbert Wabnig, since cheese contains fat, and wine is basically water, there is an obvious problem: water and fat do not mix well. So how do you guarantee a velvety fondue? Use natural and well-aged Swiss cheeses that will melt smoothly. Be sure to select a sufficiently dry white wine that will blend successfully with the cheese. If these basic ingredients are used, you will never encounter a lumpy or stringy fondue again.

INGREDIENTS

2 POUNDS SWISS CHEESE, GRATED (EMMENTALER, GRUYERE, AND APPENZELLER ARE RECOMMENDED)

1 TABLESPOON FLOUR

1 GARLIC CLOVE, HALVED

1 ½ CUPS DRY WHITE WINE

3 TABLESPOONS KIRSCH

1 TABLESPOON LEMON JUICE

PEPPER AND NUTMEG, TO TASTE

2 LOAVES OF CRUSTY ITALIAN OR FRENCH BREAD, CUT INTO CUBES

DIRECTIONS

1. Dredge the cheese in the flour.

2. Rub the inside of your fondue pot with the halves of the garlic clove. Add the white wine and kirsch. Heat on stovetop over medium heat until the wine is hot but not boiling. Add lemon juice.

3. Add handfuls of cheese, stirring constantly with a wooden spoon until the cheese is melted. The mixture should have the appearance of a light, creamy sauce. Season with pepper and nutmeg.

4. Bring to a boil, then remove the pot from heat. Place on a lit fondue burner on your table and enjoy.

PRO TIP: To thicken a thin fondue, add a little bit of cheese dabbed with flour. Mix well while it is melting. To lighten a thick fondue, add some lukewarm wine and mix well again.

VERMONT
CREAMERY

ALLISON HOOPER AND BOB REESE STARTED THE
award-winning Vermont Creamery over 30 years ago, and since then the company's output
has grown to include cow's milk, goat, and aged cheeses, as well as cream and butter. Adeline
Druart, President of Vermont Creamery, thinks the cheese board is the essence of their
company: "There is something so wonderful about arranging some beautiful cheese on a
board with whatever fruit or vegetables happen to be in season and creating something that
is both visually appealing and delicious at the same time. Making a board is also incredibly
inclusive and it always creates conversation, which is really nice when you are entertaining."

*A note on all Vermont Creamery recipes: These recipes have been adapted since not everyone
can get Vermont Creamery products. But if you have access to them we wholly endorse
using them!

Baked St. Albans

YIELD: **4 TO 6 SERVINGS**

ACTIVE TIME: **10 MINUTES**

TOTAL TIME: **30 MINUTES**

This recipe is the Vermont Creamery's take on a traditional baked Brie that comes around during the holiday season. A spoonful of fruit jam adorns the top of this rich and creamy cheese and a sheet of puff pastry covers its rind. Some time in the oven transforms this already creamy cheese into a wonder.

INGREDIENTS

1 PACKAGE OF VERMONT
  CREAMERY ST. ALBANS (OR A
  SIMILAR SOFT COW'S MILK
  CHEESE LIKE BRIE
  OR SAINT-MARCELLIN)

1 TABLESPOON RASPBERRY JAM

1 SHEET OF PUFF PASTRY, THAWED

1 BAGUETTE, SLICED

DIRECTIONS

1. Preheat oven to 350°F.

2. Spoon the jam onto the top of the cheese.

3. Cut the sheet of puff pastry into a square slightly larger than the crock that the cheese comes in. Dampen the bottom edge of the sheet with water, then gently lay it over the cheese, pressing down to seal.

4. Place the crock on a baking sheet or in a baking dish. Bake for 20 minutes, or until pastry is lightly brown and crispy.

5. Serve immediately with the sliced baguette.

Herb-Marinated Goat Cheese

YIELD: **4 TO 6 SERVINGS**

ACTIVE TIME: **10 MINUTES**

TOTAL TIME: **1 HOUR 10 MINUTES**

This herb-marinated goat cheese will travel well and is perfect for a picnic. A selection of fresh seasonal herbs soaked in olive oil infuse the goat cheese with deliciously vibrant flavors, while still allowing the cheese's tanginess to shine through.

INGREDIENTS

8 OZ. FRESH GOAT CHEESE

⅓ CUP FRESH HERBS, CHOPPED (TARRAGON, CHIVES, AND THYME ARE RECOMMENDED)

1 CUP EXTRA VIRGIN OLIVE OIL

GRILLED BREAD OR CRACKERS

DIRECTIONS

1. Remove fresh goat cheese logs from wrapper and slice into thick rounds.

2. Gently roll cheese rounds in the herbs and press so that the herbs adhere to the surface of the cheese.

3. Layer the goat cheese rounds in glass jars. Pour olive oil over the cheese until it's almost covered.

4. Let marinate for an hour before serving with grilled bread or crackers. Can be stored for up to a week in the fridge.

PRO TIP: You can include roasted garlic cloves or a pinch of red pepper flakes to boost the flavor.

Goat Cheese-Stuffed Peppadew Peppers

YIELD: **4 TO 6 SERVINGS**

ACTIVE TIME: **5 MINUTES**

TOTAL TIME: **1 HOUR**

These are an easy-to-prepare, no-frills fan favorite on a cheese board, or served amongst tapas at a summer gathering. The sweet and tart peppers pair perfectly with the creaminess of spreadable goat cheese. This dish stores well in the fridge, so it can be prepared ahead of time.

INGREDIENTS

4 OZ. SPREADABLE GOAT CHEESE

6 OZ. PEPPADEW PEPPERS

2 TABLESPOONS EXTRA VIRGIN OLIVE OIL

4 TABLESPOONS BASIL, CHOPPED

GRILLED BREAD OR CRACKERS

DIRECTIONS

1. Stir the spreadable goat cheese. Then, spoon into either a piping bag with a small round tip or a sandwich bag with a small hole cut into one corner.

2. Drain the peppadew peppers, but don't rinse.

3. Using the piping or sandwich bag, fill each pepper with goat cheese and place them on a plate.

4. Once all the peppers are filled, drizzle olive oil on top and sprinkle with the basil. Serve with grilled bread or crackers.

CHAPTER 4:

BOARDS

FOR ALL

SEASONS

Filled with dizzying arrays of hard and soft cheeses, in-season fruits, pungent cured meats, creamy dips, and punchy pickles, a thoughtfully arranged, bountiful serving board can appeal to and satisfy anyone. They become centerpieces of social gatherings, causing us to gather and talk as we enjoy what's on offer. Serving boards are informal but can be fancy; they can be a collection of snacks or a carefully composed meal.

They are whatever you want to make them. What follows are arrestingly beautiful boards created by Vermont Creamery that can either be emulated or used as the inspiration for your own medley.

Spring Board for Success

YIELD: **4 TO 6 SERVINGS**

ACTIVE TIME: **5 MINUTES**

TOTAL TIME: **1 HOUR**

When the ground has thawed but there's still a chill in the air, you want to capture the excitement of renewal and ensure that no one leaves hungry. This lovely blend of light and hearty bites has you covered.

INGREDIENTS

ASSORTED GOAT CHEESES

ASSORTED AGED CHEESES

CHARCUTERIE (SUCH AS HARD SALAMI, PROSCIUTTO, AND SOPPRESSATA)

FRESH VEGETABLES (SUCH AS SNOW PEAS, BROCCOLI, AND CELERY)

PICKLED ASPARAGUS (SEE PAGE 149)

HERB-ROASTED ALMONDS (SEE PAGE 134)

MURRAY'S CHEESE BEER CHEESE (SEE PAGE 74)

BLACK OLIVE TAPENADE (SEE PAGE 165)

PICKLED BEETS (SEE PAGE 150)

RUSTIC BAKERY FETA AND HERB QUICKBREAD (SEE PAGE 55)

DIRECTIONS

1. Take cheeses out of the fridge 1 hour prior to serving and allow to come to room temperature.

2. Arrange the ingredients on a serving board.

Summer Antipasto Cheeseboard

YIELD: **4 TO 6 SERVINGS**

ACTIVE TIME: **5 MINUTES**

TOTAL TIME: **1 HOUR**

The last thing you want to do in the summer is stand around a hot kitchen. This board will get you out with your friends and family and keep you cool.

INGREDIENTS

ASSORTED FRESH GOAT CHEESES

ASSORTED AGED CHEESES

GOAT CHEESE–STUFFED PEPPADEW
    PEPPERS (SEE PAGE 86)

HERB-MARINATED GOAT
    CHEESE (SEE PAGE 85)

CHARCUTERIE
    (SUCH AS HARD SALAMI,
    PROSCIUTTO, AND SPECK)

NUTS, ROASTED
    (MARCONA ALMONDS AND
    PECANS WORK WELL)

FRESH VEGETABLES
    (TOMATOES AND CUCUMBERS
    ARE GOOD OPTIONS)

GRILLED BREAD AND PITA WEDGES

HUMMUS

PEPERONCINI

ASSORTED OLIVES

HONEY

DIRECTIONS

1. Take cheeses out of the fridge 1 hour prior to serving and allow to come to room temperature.

2. Arrange the ingredients on a serving board.

Festive Fall Cheeseboard

YIELD: **4 TO 6 SERVINGS**

ACTIVE TIME: **5 MINUTES**

TOTAL TIME: **1 HOUR**

Fall means watching football for many, and this lovely board allows you to please everyone without having to run around the kitchen all morning.

INGREDIENTS

ASSORTED FRESH GOAT CHEESES

ASSORTED AGED CHEESES

CHARCUTERIE
   (SUCH AS HARD SALAMI,
   PROSCIUTTO, AND SPECK)

NUTS, ROASTED
   (MARCONA ALMONDS AND
   PECANS WORK WELL)

FRESH OR DRIED FRUIT (CITRUS,
   GRAPES, DRIED APRICOTS,
   DATES, FIGS, AND CURRANTS
   ARE GOOD OPTIONS)

1 BAGUETTE OR OTHER
   CRUSTY BREAD, SLICED

OLIVES OR CORNICHONS

HONEY

JAM

DIRECTIONS

1. Take cheeses out of the fridge 1 hour prior to serving and allow them to come to room temperature.

2. Arrange ingredients on a serving board.

'Tis the Season for Cheesin' Holiday Board

The table can get a little crowded around the holidays, which means you've got to keep your board simple but still make it count. This elegant board has you covered.

YIELD: **4 TO 6 SERVINGS**

ACTIVE TIME: **15 MINUTES**

TOTAL TIME: **15 MINUTES**

INGREDIENTS

4 OZ. FRESH GOAT CHEESE

½ CUP ROASTED NUTS, DRIED FRUIT, AND/OR FRESH HERBS TO ROLL GOAT CHEESE IN

CANDIED NUTS

CHOCOLATE TRUFFLES

BLACKBERRIES OR OTHER FRESH FRUIT

DIRECTIONS

1. Finely chop nuts, herbs, and/or fruits as desired into a consistent blend.

2. Remove goat cheese log from packaging and roll or press into your finely chpped blend.

3. Allow to come to room temperature before arranging on the board with the remaining ingredients. If preparing in advance, wrap in plastic wrap and store in refrigerator for 1 to 2 days.

CHAPTER 5

PRESERVES

& OTHER

CONDIMENTS

Preserving fruits and vegetables was born out of necessity. Before refrigeration, the only way to consume berries, stone fruits, tomatoes, and the like out of season was in a jam, jelly, or preserve. There is a difference between the three. Jelly and jam are both made by crushing the main ingredient, but jelly only uses the juice yielded from the process, while jam includes pulp. The fruit or vegetable used in a preserve isn't crushed; instead the main ingredient is chopped up and cooked with sugar and then stored in syrup or jam.

Made to be sweet, savory, or downright spicy, preserved fruits and vegetables make for ideal additions to serving boards. Pairing them with other condiments adds balance and helps accentuate all the other flavors.

Fig Jam

YIELD: **3 TO 4 CUPS**

ACTIVE TIME: **30 MINUTES**

TOTAL TIME: **1 HOUR AND 15 MINUTES**

Yes, the store has some decent options, but this fig jam is easy to make at home and you'll certainly taste the difference. It's perfect with scones, breads, and cheeses.

INGREDIENTS

2 POUNDS FIGS, STEMMED AND CUT INTO ½-INCH PIECES

1½ CUPS GRANULATED SUGAR

¼ CUP WATER

¼ CUP LEMON JUICE

PINCH OF SALT

1 VANILLA BEAN, SPLIT AND SEEDED (OPTIONAL)

1 CINNAMON STICK (OPTIONAL)

DIRECTIONS

1. Place all of the ingredients in a medium saucepan and bring to a boil. Stir occasionally until the sugar is dissolved. If you include the vanilla bean in your preparation, add the seeds and the pod.

2. Reduce heat to low. Cook while stirring occasionally, for 30 to 60 minutes or until the liquid is thick, sticky, and falls heavily from the spoon.

3. Remove pan from heat and, if using, discard the vanilla pod and cinnamon stick.

4. For a chunky jam, gently mash the large pieces of fig with a fork or potato masher. For a smoother jam, process the mixture in a food processor.

5. Spoon jam into jars, leaving ¼-inch space at the top and cover with lid. Let cool to room temperature, then refrigerate. Store the jam in the refrigerator for up to 2 months.

Cranberry Preserves

YIELD: **2 CUPS**

ACTIVE TIME: **15 MINUTES**

TOTAL TIME: **1 HOUR**

These preserves are here to save your holidays, as they'll keep you clear of the canned, store-bought cranberry sauce.

INGREDIENTS

1 (12 OZ.) BAG FRESH OR FROZEN CRANBERRIES (ABOUT 3 ½ CUPS)

1 CUP SUGAR

½ CUP FRESH ORANGE JUICE

1 CUP WATER

DIRECTIONS

1. Bring all ingredients to a boil in a large, heavy saucepan over medium heat, stirring occasionally.

2. Reduce heat. Simmer while stirring occasionally until the mixture thickens, about 20 minutes. Remove the saucepan from heat.

3. Force the mixture through a fine-mesh sieve into a bowl, discarding skins and seeds. Cool, while stirring occasionally. Serve when cooled to room temperature or store in the refrigerator for up to 4 days.

Esters Wine Shop & Bar
Strawberry-Rhubarb Chutney

YIELD: **4 CUPS**

ACTIVE TIME: **5 MINUTES**

TOTAL TIME: **30 MINUTES**

Chef Jessica Liu makes this strawberry rhubarb chutney in the spring, at the height of the season. It's a house favorite at Esters.

INGREDIENTS

2 TABLESPOONS OLIVE OIL

¼ CUP RED ONION, DICED

2 CLOVES GARLIC, GRATED
    ON A MICROPLANE

1-INCH PIECE OF GINGER,
    FINELY MINCED OR GRATED
    ON A MICROPLANE

5 RHUBARB STALKS, THINLY
    SLICED TO ¼ INCH PIECES

1 CUP WHITE WINE

3 CARDAMOM PODS, SEEDED
    AND GROUND

5 CLOVES, GROUND

1 TEASPOON BLACK
    PEPPER GROUND

¼ CUP ORGANIC CANE SUGAR

2 TABLESPOONS LIME JUICE

2 TABLESPOONS APPLE
    CIDER VINEGAR

1 PINT STRAWBERRIES

DIRECTIONS

1. In a medium size pot, heat up olive oil and then sweat the red onions for about 1 minute. Add the garlic, ginger, and rhubarb. Sweat for about 3 to 5 mins on medium heat, stirring frequently.

2. Add the white wine to deglaze, cook for about 1 minute. Add spices, sugar, lime juice, and vinegar and cook for another 2 to 5 minutes.

3. Once desired consistency for rhubarb is achieved add strawberries and cook for about 2 minutes. Check seasoning and adjust accordingly.

PRO TIP: If you would like a smoother chutney, cook for an additional 5 to 10 minutes once the strawberries have been added.

Quince Paste

This popular paste is Spanish in origin and goes particularly well with Manchego cheese.

YIELD: **2 ¼ POUNDS**

ACTIVE TIME: **40 MINUTES**

TOTAL TIME: **7 HOURS**

INGREDIENTS

4 MEDIUM QUINCES (ABOUT 2 POUNDS TOTAL)

¼ TO ½ CUP WATER

2 TO 3 CUPS SUGAR

DIRECTIONS

1. Preheat oven to 350°F and lightly oil a 1-quart terrine.

2. Scrub quinces and pat dry. Place quinces in a small baking pan and cover with foil. Place in the middle rack of the oven. Bake until tender, about 2 hours.

3. Transfer the pan to a rack to cool. Once the quinces are cool enough to handle, peel, quarter, and core the quinces using a sharp knife.

4. In a food processor, puree the quinces with ¼ cup water until smooth. If the mixture is too thick, add the remaining water a little at a time as needed. Pass the puree through a large fine sieve into a liquid measuring cup. Transfer puree to a 3-quart heavy saucepan and add an equivalent amount of sugar.

5. Cook quince puree over moderate heat. Stir constantly until it thickens and starts to pull away from the side of the pan, about 25 minutes. Pour puree into a terrine, smooth the top with an offset spatula, and cool. Loosely cover in plastic wrap and chill until set, about 4 hours.

6. Run a knife around sides of terrine and invert quince paste onto a platter. Quince paste, if wrapped in waxed paper and plastic wrap, can be kept chilled for 3 months.

7. Slice paste before serving.

Blood Orange Marmalade

This vibrant preserve adds color and considerable flavor to any serving board.

YIELD: 6 CUPS

ACTIVE TIME: 20 MINUTES

TOTAL TIME: 1 HOUR AND 30 MINUTES

INGREDIENTS

2 POUNDS BLOOD ORANGES

3 TABLESPOONS FRESH
    LEMON JUICE

4 CUPS SUGAR

DIRECTIONS

1. Using vegetable peeler, carefully remove the peels from 3 or 4 oranges. Remove any white pith from the peels with a sharp knife. Cut peels into extremely thin slices and set aside.

2. Peel the remaining blood oranges and discard the peels. Remove the membranes and seeds from the oranges, then cut into small cubes.

3. In a 3-quart saucepan, place orange segments, lemon juice, and sugar. Bring to a boil over medium-high heat, stirring frequently. Once boiling, reduce heat to medium. Simmer for about 45 minutes until the mixture reaches 225°F on a candy thermometer.

4. Meanwhile, in a 1-quart saucepan, place orange peel slices and cover with water. Bring to a boil. Cook for about 4 minutes, then drain and set aside. Add the slices of peel to the larger saucepan during last few minutes of simmering.

5. Ladle marmalade into sterilized jars. Top with sterilized lids and rims.

6. Cool completely before storing.

Pantry Chutney

YIELD: **2 CUPS**

ACTIVE TIME: **5 MINUTES**

TOTAL TIME: **15 MINUTES**

Any combination of dried fruit will work in this chutney, and it can likely be made with items you already have in your pantry.

INGREDIENTS

1 SHALLOT, FINELY CHOPPED

1 TABLESPOON CORIANDER SEEDS

1 TABLESPOON GINGER, PEELED AND FINELY CHOPPED

1 TEASPOON VEGETABLE OIL

1½ CUPS DRIED APRICOTS, COARSELY CHOPPED

1 CUP APPLE CIDER VINEGAR

¼ CUP DRIED FIGS, COARSELY CHOPPED

¼ CUP PRUNES, COARSELY CHOPPED

¼ CUP GOLDEN RAISINS

¼ CUP DARK MOLASSES

1 ½ CUPS WATER

KOSHER SALT AND FRESHLY GROUND BLACK PEPPER, TO TASTE

DIRECTIONS

1. Combine shallot, coriander, ginger, and oil in a medium saucepan and cook over medium heat until fragrant, about 1 minute.

2. Add apricots, vinegar, figs, prunes, raisins, molasses, and the water. Season with salt and pepper.

3. Bring to a simmer and cook until fruit is soft and the liquid is almost completely evaporated. If the mixture becomes too thick, you can add more water to thin it out. Let cool, cover, and store in the refrigerator for up to 1 week.

Apricot and Chili Jam

YIELD: **8 CUPS**

ACTIVE TIME: **20 MINUTES**

TOTAL TIME: **1 HOUR AND 30 MINUTES**

This spicy jam pairs nicely with Brie, as well as a variety of goat cheeses.

INGREDIENTS

- 2 POUNDS OF APRICOTS
- 1 SMALL LEMON
- 2 POUNDS WHITE SUGAR
- 1 CUP WATER
- 3 OR 4 RED CHILIES, ACCORDING TO TASTE
- 1 TABLESPOON BUTTER OR MARGARINE

DIRECTIONS

1. Wash and dry all of the apricots. Cut in half and remove the stones from the center. Slice the fruit into smaller pieces and add to a large saucepan. Add the zest and juice of one lemon, the sugar, and the water.

2. Finely chop the chilies. If desired, you can blend the chilies in a food processor instead. Add the chopped chilies and their seeds into the saucepan and mix with the apricots. Slowly bring the mixture to a boil.

3. Stir gently until all of the sugar has dissolved. Allow the mixture to hold a rapid boil for a few minutes.

4. Reduce the heat to a simmer and cook for 15 to 20 minutes, stirring constantly to prevent the mixture from burning. If you prefer a chunkier jam, make sure to stir gently so that the chunks of fruit stay intact. If you want a smoother jam, mash the mixture as you stir.

5. To test your jam, remove a spoonful and drop it onto a chilled saucer. If a skin doesn't begin to form after a minute, continue simmering and testing.

6. If the jam feels like a soft jelly and has started to form a thin skin, remove the pan from the heat. Add the butter and stir to disperse any froth. Cool for 15 minutes, then fill your sterilized glass jam jars. Allow to cool completely before storing in the refrigerator.

Flavored Honey

YIELD: **1 CUP**

ACTIVE TIME: **5 MINUTES**

TOTAL TIME: **5 DAYS TO 2 WEEKS**

Infusing honey with herbs, vegetables, or flowers allows it to partner with a dizzying array of serving boards.

INGREDIENTS

1 TO 2 OZ. DRIED HERBS,
  VEGETABLES, OR FLOWERS

1 CUP HONEY

DIRECTIONS

1. Whatever you choose to infuse the honey with, keep in mind that the smaller the pieces of it are, the more difficult it will be to strain out. For instance, if you're using herbs or flowers, I'd recommend using them whole or separating them into their stems, leaves, and/or buds.

2. Place infusing element in the bottom of a jar. Then, fill the jar almost to the top with honey. Using a chopstick or other implement, coat the infusing element with honey. Fill the jar with more honey, then wipe the rim with a clean cloth and cover tightly.

3. Let the mixture infuse for at least 5 days. If the infusing element floats to the top, turn the jar over to keep them well coated. For a more intense flavor, infuse for up to 2 weeks.

4. Strain the honey into a clean jar. Depending on the volume of the mixture and the size of the strainer, you may need to do this in stages.

5. Secure the jar's lid tightly and store in a cool, dry place. It will last indefinitely.

PRO TIP: Label the jar with the ingredients to make it easier to work with later on.

Green Tomato Jam

This colorful jam is a great way to utilize an overabundance of green tomatoes and allow tomato season to be enjoyed any time of the year.

YIELD: 6 CUPS

ACTIVE TIME: 20 MINUTES

TOTAL TIME: 16 HOURS

INGREDIENTS

3 POUNDS GREEN TOMATOES

1 LEMON

1 POUND SUGAR

DIRECTIONS

1. Wash the tomatoes and pat dry. Remove the core, chop into small pieces, and remove the seeds. Place the tomato pieces in a large, nonreactive pot with a heavy bottom.

2. Zest the lemon. Keep the zest refrigerated in a small bowl with a small amount of lemon juice to keep it hydrated. Add the sugar and the juice of half the lemon in the pot. Toss, cover, and place in the refrigerator to macerate overnight.

3. In the morning, place the pot with the green tomatoes over medium-high heat. The tomatoes should have given off a fair amount of liquid overnight. Bring to a boil, stirring occasionally to avoid scorching.

4. Lower the heat so that the tomatoes are gently boiling, and cook for about an hour, stirring occasionally. Once the mixture pulls away from the pot's walls when stirred, remove from the heat and add the lemon zest.

5. With an immersion blender, puree the mixture thoroughly. Alternatively, use a regular blender, mixing in small batches until fully combined.

6. Pour the jam into clean jars and allow to cool to room temperature. Seal and store in the refrigerator for up to 3 weeks, or in the freezer for up to 3 months.

Publican Green Chile Chow Chow

YIELD: **8 CUPS**

ACTIVE TIME: **5 MINUTES**

TOTAL TIME: **40 MINUTES**

Joe Frietz of Publican Quality Market serves this simple garden of delight on most of his serving boards, noting that the fresh Hatch chilis define this condiment.

INGREDIENTS

4 CUPS DISTILLED VINEGAR

1 TABLESPOON MUSTARD POWDER

½ CUP YELLOW MUSTARD SEEDS

1 CUP SUGAR

2 BAY LEAVES

1 BUNCH OF CILANTRO,
   STEMS ONLY, CHOPPED

2 (27 OZ.) CANS HATCH
   GREEN CHILIES

½ CUP DIJON MUSTARD

SALT, TO TASTE

HATCH CHILI POWDER, TO TASTE

DIRECTIONS

1. Combine vinegar, mustard powder, mustard seeds, sugar, bay leaves, and cilantro in a medium saucepan. Cook until reduced by one-third. Add chilies and cook for another 5 minutes.

2. Add the Dijon mustard. Season with salt and remove the pan from heat.

3. Cool until the mixture starts to look gelatinous.

Publican Beer Mustard

YIELD: **4 CUPS**

ACTIVE TIME: **5 MINUTES**

TOTAL TIME: **1 HOUR**

Joe Frietze's beer mustard is as simple as it gets. Why? "You never want to outshine your meat selection," he says.

INGREDIENTS

2 CUPS YELLOW MUSTARD SEED

½ CUP BROWN MUSTARD SEED

3 CUPS MALT VINEGAR

4 CUPS BEER

¾ CUP HONEY

1 CUP BROWN SUGAR

1 TABLESPOON SALT

½ CUP DRY MUSTARD

5 ALLSPICE BERRIES, GROUND

½ CUP MUNICH MALT, GROUND

DIRECTIONS

1. Place all ingredients in a large saucepan and cook over medium heat until the seeds are soft.

2. Transfer to a food processor and puree until it achieves the desired texture. Let cool before serving.

Cilantro-Mint Chutney

YIELD: **2 CUPS**

ACTIVE TIME: **5 MINUTES**

TOTAL TIME: **5 MINUTES**

Typically served with Indian food, this chutney can be used to add a little zing to milder cheeses like mozzarella.

INGREDIENTS

2 CUPS PACKED FRESH CILANTRO SPRIGS, PACKED

1 CUP FRESH MINT LEAVES, PACKED

½ CUP WHITE ONION, CHOPPED

⅓ CUP WATER

1 TABLESPOON FRESH LIME JUICE

1 TEASPOON GREEN CHILI, CHOPPED (SERRANO OR THAI ARE GOOD OPTIONS; INCLUDE THE SEEDS OR ADJUST TO YOUR TASTE)

1 TEASPOON SUGAR

¾ TEASPOON SALT, OR TO TASTE

DIRECTIONS

1. Place all ingredients in a blender and puree. Take care not to over-puree the mixture. You want the chutney to have some texture.

Mostarda

YIELD: **½ CUP**

ACTIVE TIME: **5 MINUTES**

TOTAL TIME: **15 MINUTES**

Perfect to serve alongside cured meat, this northern Italian condiment is made from candied fruit and a thick, mustard-flavored syrup.

INGREDIENTS

¼ POUND DRIED APRICOTS, ROUGHLY CHOPPED

¼ CUP DRIED CHERRIES, ROUGHLY CHOPPED

1 SHALLOT, MINCED

1 ½ TEASPOONS CRYSTALLIZED GINGER, MINCED

½ CUP DRY WHITE WINE

3 TABLESPOONS WHITE WINE VINEGAR

3 TABLESPOONS WATER

3 TABLESPOONS SUGAR

1 TEASPOON DRIED MUSTARD

1 TEASPOON DIJON MUSTARD

1 TABLESPOON UNSALTED BUTTER

DIRECTIONS

1. In a small saucepan, combine the apricots, cherries, shallot, ginger, wine, vinegar, water, and sugar and bring to a boil. Cover and cook over medium heat until all of the liquid is absorbed and the fruit is soft, about 10 minutes.

2. Stir in the dried mustard, Dijon mustard, and butter. Simmer until the mixture is jam-like, about 2 to 3 minutes.

3. Serve warm or at room temperature, or store in the refrigerator for up to 1 week.

Homemade Horseradish

YIELD: **1 CUP**

ACTIVE TIME: **5 MINUTES**

TOTAL TIME: **5 MINUTES**

This spicy accompaniment can be served by itself or added to a variety of recipes to add a punch. It pairs perfectly with cured meat and a selection of subtle cheeses.

INGREDIENTS

1 CUP HORSERADISH ROOT, PEELED AND CHOPPED

¾ CUP WHITE VINEGAR

2 TEASPOONS WHITE SUGAR

¼ TEASPOON SALT

DIRECTIONS

1. Place all of the ingredients in a blender or food processor and puree until smooth. Carefully remove the cover of the processor or blender, keeping your face away from the container.

2. Transfer to a jar, cover, and store in the refrigerator until ready to serve.

Jalapeño Pepper Jam

YIELD: **5 TO 6 CUPS**

ACTIVE TIME: **20 MINUTES**

TOTAL TIME: **12 TO 24 HOURS**

If jalapeños aren't your favorite, feel free to substitute your preferred chili pepper. Should you want a mild jam, Anaheim peppers are a good choice.

INGREDIENTS

1 CUP GREEN BELL PEPPER, SEEDED AND MINCED OR GROUND

¼ CUP JALAPEÑO PEPPER, SEEDED TO TASTE AND MINCED OR GROUND

4 CUPS SUGAR

1 CUP APPLE CIDER VINEGAR

1 (6 OZ.) PACKET OF LIQUID FRUIT PECTIN

3 TO 5 DROPS OF GREEN FOOD COLORING (OPTIONAL)

DIRECTIONS

1. Combine peppers, sugar, and vinegar in a large nonreactive saucepan. Bring to a boil and cook for 5 minutes.

2. Remove from heat and let cool for 1 hour.

3. Add the pectin and the food coloring, if desired. Return to heat. Bring to a rolling boil and cook for 1 minute. Pour into hot, sterilized half-pint canning jars, filling to within ½ inch of the top.

4. Wipe tops of the jars. Center lids on top and make sure to screw the bands on firmly.

5. Fill a canning kettle or a large pot with a bottom rack with water and bring to a boil. Gently lower jars into water. The water should cover the jars by at least 1 inch.

6. Bring water to a full boil. Reduce heat to a gentle boil, then cover and cook for 5 minutes.

7. Carefully remove the jars from the water using tongs or a jar-lifter.

8. Place upside-down on a rack or thick towels and let cool without moving for 12 to 24 hours.

9. The jars will make popping sounds if sealed properly. Once cool, check the seal on each jar by pressing down on lid. If it doesn't push down, it's sealed. If it does push down, store in refrigerator. Otherwise, store in a cool, dark place for up to 1 year.

10. To serve, stir to soften. Then, pour over an 8 oz. block of cream cheese and spread on crackers.

Garlic and Dill Mustard

YIELD: **½ CUP**

ACTIVE TIME: **5 MINUTES**

TOTAL TIME: **2 TO 3 DAYS**

Thanks to the garlic and dill, this simple mustard can dress up any charcuterie.

INGREDIENTS

FOR BROWN MUSTARD:

½ CUP MUSTARD SEEDS

½ CUP BEER

⅓ CUP WATER

1 TABLESPOON GARLIC, MINCED

1 TABLESPOON DILL, MINCED

3 TABLESPOONS APPLE
    CIDER VINEGAR

1 TABLESPOON MAPLE SYRUP

FOR YELLOW MUSTARD:

½ CUP MUSTARD SEEDS

½ CUP WHITE WINE

1 TABLESPOON GARLIC, MINCED

1 TABLESPOON DILL, MINCED

⅓ CUP WHITE WINE VINEGAR

1 TABLESPOON SUGAR

DIRECTIONS

1. Combine ingredients of chosen mustard in a stainless-steel bowl. Cover and let stand for 2 to 3 days.

2. Pour the mixture in a blender and blend until just a little grainy.

3. If the mustard is too thick, add water 1 tablespoon at a time until you reach your desired consistency.

NOTE: This mustard will keep for up to 6 months if refrigerated in an airtight container.

CHAPTER 6:

NUTS, OLIVES & PICKLES

When most of us think of savory serving boards, we think of cured meats and creamy cheeses. But you need something to counter all that richness, which is where nuts, olives, and pickles come in. All three are a great way to inject a touch of lightness and different flavors into your spread, providing your board with a balance that will be welcomed by all.

Herb-Roasted Almonds

YIELD: **2 CUPS**

ACTIVE TIME: **10 MINUTES**

TOTAL TIME: **30 MINUTES**

Roasted almonds stand alone great on their own, but are enhanced by the flavors imparted by the fresh herbs.

INGREDIENTS

1 ½ TEASPOONS WATER

½ TEASPOON SALT

2 CUPS WHOLE RAW ALMONDS

3 THYME SPRIGS, LEAVES ONLY

1 SPRIG SAVORY, LEAVES ONLY

2 TEASPOONS OLIVE OIL

DIRECTIONS

1. Preheat oven to 375°F

2. Dissolve salt in water.

3. Add salt water to almonds and herbs.

4. Place almonds in single layer on sheet pan and roast for 15 to 20 minutes, stirring every 5 minutes. Once almonds brown remove them from the oven immediately.

5. Toss in olive oil and season to taste.

Maple Candied Walnuts

YIELD: **2 CUPS**

ACTIVE TIME: **15 MINUTES**

TOTAL TIME: **45 MINUTES**

The sweet crunch of these snacks go great with creamy cheeses and fatty cured meats.

INGREDIENTS

1 TABLESPOON UNSALTED BUTTER

2 CUPS WALNUT HALVES

⅓ CUP MAPLE SYRUP

⅛ TEASPOON SALT

DIRECTIONS

1. Preheat oven to 375 degrees.

2. Melt butter in pan over medium heat. Stir in maple syrup and salt. Simmer for about 3 minutes, until mixture is frothy.

3. Add walnuts and coat, using a rubber spatula. Cook, stirring, for about 3 minutes.

4. Place walnuts in a single layer on a parchment-lined baking sheet and bake until walnuts are caramelized, about 10 minutes.

5. Stir and let cool and harden, about 30 minutes.

Spiced Nut Mix

YIELD: **3 CUPS**

ACTIVE TIME: **10 MINUTES**

TOTAL TIME: **30 MINUTES**

This recipe is wonderful for its flexibility, as it can handle any amount of spice.

INGREDIENTS

3 TABLESPOONS BUTTER

1 (15 TO 16 OZ.) CAN OF MIXED NUTS

¼ TEASPOON WORCESTERSHIRE SAUCE

½ TEASPOON SALT

¼ TEASPOON PAPRIKA

¼ TEASPOON CAYENNE PEPPER

¼ TEASPOON CHILI POWDER

⅛ TEASPOON GROUND CUMIN

DIRECTIONS

1. In a large skillet, melt butter over low heat. Add nuts and Worcestershire sauce and cook, while stirring, for 5 to 7 minutes, or until the nuts are fragrant.

2. Remove the nuts with a slotted spoon and briefly let them drain on paper towels before transferring to a large bowl.

3. Combine remaining ingredients. Sprinkle over nuts and toss to coat. Set aside and let cool.

4. Let cool to room temperature before serving or storing in an airtight container.

Smoked and Spicy Almonds

YIELD: **2 CUPS**

ACTIVE TIME: **10 MINUTES**

TOTAL TIME: **45 MINUTES**

These nuts can be stored in an airtight container for up to 1 month, but there's almost no chance they'll last that long.

INGREDIENTS

4 TABLESPOONS BUTTER, MELTED

4 TEASPOONS WORCESTERSHIRE SAUCE

1 TEASPOON CUMIN

2 TEASPOONS CHILI POWDER

1 TEASPOON GARLIC POWDER

½ TEASPOON ONION POWDER

1 TEASPOON CAYENNE PEPPER

1 TEASPOON SALT

2 CUPS WHOLE ALMONDS

DIRECTIONS

1. Preheat oven to 350°F.

2. Line a baking sheet with parchment paper.

3. In a large bowl combine butter, Worcestershire sauce, cumin, chili powder, garlic powder, onion powder, cayenne pepper, and salt.

4. Add almonds and toss to coat with butter mixture.

5. Transfer the almonds to the baking sheet and bake for 15 to 20 minutes, or until the almonds are golden brown and fragrant. Remove the sheet and flip the nuts regularly as they cook.

6. Remove from oven and let cool before serving or storing in an airtight container.

Chipotle Peanuts

YIELD: **1 CUP**

ACTIVE TIME: **10 MINUTES**

TOTAL TIME: **30 MINUTES**

If you know your group loves milder cheeses, make sure these spicy treats make their way onto your board.

INGREDIENTS

1 CUP PEANUTS, SKINS REMOVED

1 TEASPOON CHIPOTLE POWDER

⅛ TEASPOON CAYENNE PEPPER

1 TABLESPOON LIME JUICE

1 TEASPOON LIME ZEST

½ TABLESPOON VEGETABLE OIL

1 TEASPOON SALT

DIRECTIONS

1. Preheat oven to 300°F. Place peanuts on a lined baking sheet and cook for 10 to 15 minutes, or until they are golden brown and fragrant.

2. Place the remaining ingredients in a bowl and stir until well combined. Add the peanuts and stir to combine.

3. Place on parchment paper to dry and cool.

Elevated Party Mix

YIELD: **12 CUPS**

ACTIVE TIME: **15 MINUTES**

TOTAL TIME: **1 HOUR AND 30 MINUTES**

A hot-and-spicy take on a bonafide classic. Don't be shy about substituting your favorites for what's suggested here.

INGREDIENTS

6 CUPS CHEX

1 CUP PRETZEL TWISTS OR STICKS

1 CUP SESAME STICKS (TYPICALLY FOUND IN THE BULK FOOD AREA AT A HEALTH FOOD OR GROCERY STORE)

1 CUP WHITE CHEDDAR CHEESE CRACKERS

1 CUP CASHEWS

1 CUP PECANS

½ CUP SESAME SEEDS

¾ CUP UNSALTED BUTTER

1 ½ TABLESPOONS SOY SAUCE

2 TEASPOONS GARAM MASALA

2 TEASPOONS CURRY POWDER

1 TEASPOON SUGAR

1 TEASPOON CAYENNE PEPPER

DIRECTIONS

1. Preheat oven to 250°F.

2. Line two baking sheets with parchment paper.

3. Combine chex, pretzels, sesame sticks, crackers, nuts, and sesame seeds in a large bowl.

4. Place the remaining ingredients in a medium saucepan and cook over medium heat until the butter is melted.

5. Stir the butter mixture and then pour it over the cereal mixture. Stir until evenly coated.

6. Spread mixture onto prepared baking sheets and bake for 1 hour.

7. Remove from oven and let cool before serving. This mix will keep in an airtight container for 1 month.

Quick Pickles

YIELD: **2 PINTS**

ACTIVE TIME: **15 MINUTES**

TOTAL TIME: **12 HOURS TO 2 DAYS**

This forgiving, flexible, and flavorful recipe allows you to pickle any vegetable, so long as it's fresh.

INGREDIENTS

1 POUND FRESH VEGETABLES,
  SUCH AS CUCUMBERS,
  CARROTS, GREEN BEANS,
  SUMMER SQUASH,
  OR CHERRY TOMATOES

2 SPRIGS OF FRESH HERBS,
  SUCH AS THYME, DILL, OR
  ROSEMARY (OPTIONAL)

1 TO 2 TEASPOONS WHOLE SPICES,
  SUCH AS BLACK PEPPERCORNS,
  CORIANDER, OR MUSTARD
  SEEDS (OPTIONAL)

1 TEASPOON DRIED HERBS OR
  GROUND SPICES (OPTIONAL)

2 GARLIC CLOVES, SMASHED
  OR SLICED (OPTIONAL)

1 CUP VINEGAR, SUCH AS WHITE,
  APPLE CIDER, OR RICE

1 CUP WATER

1 TABLESPOON KOSHER SALT OR
  2 TEASPOONS PICKLING SALT

1 TABLESPOON GRANULATED
  SUGAR (OPTIONAL)

DIRECTIONS

1. Wash 2 wide-mouth pint jars, lids, and bands in warm soapy water and rinse well. Set aside to dry, or dry by hand.

2. Wash and dry the vegetables. Peel carrots, if using. Trim the ends of the green beans, if using. Cut vegetables into desired shapes and sizes.

3. Divide whatever herbs, spices, and/or garlic you are using evenly between the jars.

4. Pack the vegetables into the jars, making sure there is a ½ inch of space remaining at the top. Pack them in as tightly as you can without damaging the vegetables.

5. Combine the vinegar, water, and salt in a small saucepan and cook over high heat. If using, add the sugar. Bring to a boil, stirring to dissolve the salt and sugar. Pour the brine over the vegetables, filling each jar to within ½ inch of the top. You may not use all the brine.

6. Gently tap the jars against the counter a few times to remove all the air bubbles. Top off with more pickling brine if necessary.

7. Place the lids on the jars and screw on the bands until tight.

8. Let the jars cool to room temperature. Store the pickles in the refrigerator. The pickles will improve with flavor as they age, so try to wait at least 48 hours before cracking them open.

Dilly Beans

YIELD: **5 PINTS**

ACTIVE TIME: **10 MINUTES**

TOTAL TIME: **1 WEEK**

These crunchy and flavorful beans look great on any board. Be sure not to overcook them; you want to retain that crunch.

INGREDIENTS

3 POUNDS GREEN BEANS

2 ½ CUPS WHITE VINEGAR

2 ½ CUPS WATER

4 TABLESPOONS PICKLING SALT

5 MEDIUM GARLIC CLOVES

5 TEASPOONS DILL SEEDS
   (NOT DILL WEED)

5 TEASPOONS RED PEPPER FLAKES

DIRECTIONS

1. Prepare a boiling water bath and 5 pint jars. Place lids and bands in a small saucepan and simmer over low heat while you prepare the beans.

2. Wash and trim the beans so that they fit in jar. If you have particularly long beans, cut them in half. Combine vinegar, water, and salt in a medium saucepan and bring to a boil.

3. While the pickling liquid heats, pack your beans into the jars, leaving ½ inch of space free at the top.

4. Place 1 clove of garlic, 1 teaspoon dill seeds, and 1 teaspoon red pepper flakes in each jar.

5. Slowly pour the hot brine over the beans, leaving ½ inch from the top free. After the jars are full, use a wooden chopstick to remove the air bubbles. Add more brine if necessary.

6. Wipe the rims, apply lids and bands, and process in the hot water bath for 10 minutes. Let beans sit for at least 1 week before serving.

Pickled Okra

YIELD: **2 PINTS**

ACTIVE TIME: **15 MINUTES**

TOTAL TIME: **1 HOUR**

Okra, which is also known as ladies' fingers, pickles well and looks great piled up on a board.

INGREDIENTS

1 POUND OKRA, TRIMMED

4 SMALL DRIED RED CHILIES

2 BAY LEAVES

2 GARLIC CLOVES, HALVED

1 TEASPOON DILL SEEDS

1 TEASPOON CORIANDER SEEDS

1 TEASPOON BLACK PEPPERCORNS

1 ½ CUPS WATER

1 ½ CUPS CIDER VINEGAR

1 ½ TABLESPOONS KOSHER SALT

DIRECTIONS

1. In a large saucepan, bring 6 cups of water to a boil. This will serve as your bath once the jars have been closed.

2. Pack the okra, chilies, bay leaves, and garlic cloves into 2 sterilized, 1-pint canning jars. Divide the dill seeds, coriander seeds, and peppercorns evenly between each jar.

3. In a medium saucepan, combine the water, vinegar, and salt and bring to a boil over high heat, stirring to dissolve the salt.

4. Pour the brine over the okra, leaving a ½ inch of space at the top. Apply the lids and bands.

5. Place the jars in the boiling water and boil for 10 minutes. Remove, let cool to room temperature, and serve immediately. Can be stored in a cool, dark place for up to 1 year. Refrigerate after opening.

Pickled Asparagus

YIELD: **6 PINTS**

ACTIVE TIME: **15 MINUTES**

TOTAL TIME: **60 MINUTES**

If you can, get your hands on the freshest asparagus you can find; it makes a great difference in flavor.

INGREDIENTS

3 POUNDS ASPARAGUS,
    WOODY ENDS REMOVED

2 TO 3 SPRIGS OF
    FRESH DILL WEED

2 ½ CUPS WHITE VINEGAR

2 ½ CUPS WATER

¼ CUP PICKLING SALT

1 TABLESPOON DILL SEEDS

2 TEASPOONS CORIANDER SEEDS

2 TEASPOONS MUSTARD SEEDS

1 TEASPOON ALLSPICE BERRIES

2 TABLESPOONS CANE SUGAR

4 GARLIC CLOVES, MINCED

DIRECTIONS

1. Cut the asparagus to fit the length of whatever jars you're using, leaving ¼ inch of space free at the top of the jars. Pack the asparagus into the jars as tightly as you can. Tuck the fresh dill weed in between the asparagus.

2. To make the brine, place all remaining ingredients into a medium saucepan and bring to a boil. Boil for 3 minutes.

3. Pour the hot brine into the jars, making sure to get some of the seeds and garlic in each jar. Leave ¼ inch of space free at the top of each jar. Screw the lids on tightly.

4. Once the jars have cooled, refrigerate them for at least a week before eating. The asparagus can be stored in the refrigerator for around a month.

5. If you want to can these for long-term storage, immediately after pouring in the hot liquid and sealing the jars, process the jars in a boiling water bath for 10 minutes. Remove the jars and let them sit undisturbed for 24 hours before moving them. These will keep for up to a year.

Pickled Beets

YIELD: **4 PINTS**

ACTIVE TIME: **30 MINUTES**

TOTAL TIME: **2 HOURS**

This recipe works with any type of beet, but candy-striped beets look fantastic pickled in the jar and even better on a board. And keep in mind that red will stain a serving board and your guests' fingers.

INGREDIENTS

4 POUNDS BEETS

2 ½ CUPS WHITE VINEGAR

1 ¼ CUP WATER

1 ¼ CUP SUGAR

1 TEASPOON PICKLING SALT

2 SMALL ONIONS, THINLY SLICED

DIRECTIONS

1. Scrub and trim beets, leaving a small section of the stem. Bring water to boil in a large saucepan, add the beets, and reduce the heat to a simmer. Cook for 30 minutes, or until beets are tender. Remove and let beets cool. Rinse and quarter the beets, while taking care to preserve the stem. When served on a board, in a bowl, or in a nice pile, the stem gives you something to grab onto, making utensils unnecessary.

2. Place the vinegar, water, sugar, and salt in a Dutch oven, bring to a boil, and then add the beets and onions. Reduce heat and let simmer for 5 to 10 minutes.

3. Pour mixture into hot jars, packing tightly. Pour additional liquid over the beets and onions leaving about ½ inch of space free at the top. Wipe jars clean, attach lids, apply bands, and screw on until tight.

4. In a large saucepan, bring 6 cups of water to a boil. This will serve as your bath once the jars have been closed. Place the jars in the bath for 30 minutes and then turn off the heat and let the jars stand for 5 to 10 minutes.

Standard Pickle

ACTIVE TIME: **5 MINUTES**

TOTAL TIME: **30 MINUTES**

I prefer champagne vinegar or distilled vinegar in most contexts, but feel free to get wild and use other ones. I have used this liquid for everything from onions and carrots to bacon. And yes, pickled bacon is as awesome as it sounds. You can basically pickle whatever you want with this solution.

INGREDIENTS

2 PARTS VINEGAR

1 PART SUGAR

1 PART WATER

DIRECTIONS

1. Combine all ingredients in a saucepan and bring to a boil.

2. Add whatever you feel like pickling to the liquid. Allow the liquid to return to a boil. Cook for 1 minute.

3. Remove the saucepan from heat and allow to cool to room temperature before serving.

Pickled Tomatoes

YIELD: ½ **CUP**

ACTIVE TIME: **10 MINUTES**

TOTAL TIME: **12 HOURS AND 30 MINUTES**

In the midst of tomato season, where there are too many to know what to do with, try pickling tomatoes. Pickle whole cherry tomatoes or sliced green ones—no matter what they add a vibrant bite and color to any serving board.

INGREDIENTS

4 TABLESPOONS WHITE WINE VINEGAR

1 ½ TEASPOONS BROWN SUGAR

2 TEASPOONS SALT

½ TEASPOON GARLIC, MINCED

2 TEASPOONS MUSTARD SEEDS

¼ TEASPOON CRACKED PEPPERCORNS

1 TEASPOON CUMIN

CAYENNE PEPPER, TO TASTE

¼ TEASPOON TURMERIC

1 ½ TABLESPOONS EXTRA VIRGIN OLIVE OIL

1 TOMATO, CONCASSE AND CHOPPED

DIRECTIONS

1. Combine all ingredients except the tomato in a small saucepan. Bring to a simmer over medium heat.

2. Remove from heat and let cool.

3. Once cool, add chopped tomatoes, place in refrigerator, and allow to marinate for 12 hours.

TO CONCASSE A TOMATO:

Boil enough water for a tomato to be submerged and add a pinch of salt. While it is heating, prepare an ice bath and score the top of the tomato with a paring knife, taking care not to cut into the meat of the tomato. Place the tomato in the boiling water for 30 seconds, or until the skin begins to blister.

Carefully remove it from the boiling water and place it in the ice bath. Once the tomato is cool, remove it from the ice bath and use a paring knife to peel the skin off, starting at the scored top. Cut the tomato into quarters, remove the seeds, and cut according to instructions.

Hot and Spicy Carrots

YIELD: **1 PINT**

ACTIVE TIME: **15 MINUTES**

TOTAL TIME: **1 HOUR AND 30 MINUTES**

If you really want to dress up your serving board, use heirloom carrots and take advantage of their assorted colors.

INGREDIENTS

½ POUND DAIKON, PEELED

½ POUND LARGE CARROTS, PEELED

1 CUP UNSEASONED RICE VINEGAR

1 TEASPOON KOSHER OR SEA SALT

2 TABLESPOONS SUGAR,
    PLUS 2 TEASPOONS

1 CUP WATER

DIRECTIONS

1. Wash daikon and carrots and cut into matchsticks or rounds. The rounds should be about the size of a quarter. Pat dry.

2. In bowl, mix vinegar, salt, sugar, and water until the sugar dissolves. Add the carrots and daikon to the mixture and let marinate for at least 1 hour before serving.

3. For best flavor, store vegetables in an airtight mason jar in the refrigerator for up to 5 days.

Retro Bread and Butter Pickles

YIELD: **½ CUP**

ACTIVE TIME: **5 MINUTES**

TOTAL: **12 HOURS TO 1 WEEK**

Those who have enjoyed these pickles on one of my own boards can thank my grandmother, who passed along this wonderful recipe.

INGREDIENTS

- ½ ENGLISH HOTHOUSE CUCUMBER OR 2 PERSIAN CUCUMBERS, THINLY SLICED
- 1 SMALL ONION, THINLY SLICED
- 2 JALAPEÑO PEPPERS, THINLY SLICED
- 4 LARGE DILL SPRIGS
- 2 TABLESPOONS CORIANDER SEEDS
- 2 TABLESPOONS MUSTARD SEEDS
- 2 TEASPOONS CELERY SALT
- 2 CUPS DISTILLED WHITE VINEGAR
- 1 CUP SUGAR
- 2 TABLESPOONS KOSHER SALT

DIRECTIONS

1. Pack cucumber slices, onion, jalapeños, dill sprigs, coriander seeds, mustard seeds, and celery salt into a 1-quart jar.

2. Bring vinegar, sugar, and salt to a boil in a medium saucepan, stirring to dissolve sugar and salt. Carefully pour into jar, filling all the way to the top. Seal jar and refrigerate for at least 12 hours and up to 1 week.

Pickled Peppers

YIELD: **1 ½ CUPS**

ACTIVE TIME: **10 MINUTES**

TOTAL TIME: **1 HOUR AND 30 MINUTES**

If you use a variety of chili peppers, this recipe is another great way to add color to your board.

INGREDIENTS

2 TABLESPOONS GRAPESEED OIL

12 OZ. CHILIES

4 GARLIC CLOVES, HALVED

1 ¾ CUPS WHITE VINEGAR

¾ CUP WATER

1 TABLESPOON SUGAR

½ TEASPOON SALT

DIRECTIONS

1. In a large skillet, warm the oil over medium-high heat and add the chilies and garlic. Sauté, stirring frequently until softened, for about 5 minutes. Remove from heat and let the chilies cool until they can be handled.

2. Add the chilies and garlic to a sanitized 1-quart jar or 4 smaller mason jars. If desired, slice some of the chilies in half lengthwise in order to infuse the vinegar.

3. Place the vinegar, water, sugar, and salt in a small saucepan and cook, while stirring, until the sugar and salt are dissolved.

4. Pour the water-and-vinegar mixture over the chilies and allow the contents of the jar to cool to room temperature. Seal the jar and refrigerate for up to 1 month.

CHAPTER 7:

DIPS & SPREADS

Dips and spreads are about as versatile as it gets. Whether you're an omnivore, vegan, or gluten free, there are countless tasty preparations that fit any and all dietary requirements and tastes. It doesn't matter if you're using sliced vegetables, crackers, or bread, any of these dips and spreads can complement the contents of a serving board, or serve as the centerpiece.

Black Olive Tapenade

YIELD: **1 ½ CUPS**

ACTIVE TIME: **5 MINUTES**

TOTAL TIME: **5 MINUTES**

This spread can be made with any type of olives, but for whatever reason I find that black olives are the most pleasing to my eye.

INGREDIENTS

1 ½ CUPS PITTED,
   BRINE-CURED OLIVES

1 TEASPOON ANCHOVY PASTE OR
   2 ANCHOVY FILETS, MINCED

3 TABLESPOONS CAPERS, RINSED

1 ½ TABLESPOONS
   PARSLEY, CHOPPED

3 GARLIC CLOVES
   (ROASTING IS OPTIONAL)

3 TABLESPOONS FRESH
   LEMON JUICE

¼ TEASPOON BLACK PEPPER,
   PLUS MORE TO TASTE

¼ CUP OLIVE OIL

SALT AND PEPPER TO TASTE

DIRECTIONS

1. In a food processor, combine olives, anchovy component, capers, parsley, garlic, lemon juice, and black pepper. Pulse 2 to 3 times until coarsely chopped.

2. Drizzle in olive oil and pulse a few more times until a chunky paste forms, scraping down the sides as needed.

3. Season to taste with salt and pepper and serve at room temperature.

Sun-Dried Tomato and Pistachio Tapenade

YIELD: **1 ½ TO 2 CUPS**

ACTIVE TIME: **10 MINUTES**

TOTAL TIME: **20 MINUTES**

Everyone knows sun-dried tomatoes are divine, but pairing their sweetness with salty pistachios takes them to a level I didn't think existed.

INGREDIENTS

- ¼ CUP EXTRA VIRGIN OLIVE OIL, PLUS ONE TABLESPOON
- 1 SHALLOT, MINCED
- 1 TEASPOON DRY VERMOUTH
- ¾ CUP SUN-DRIED TOMATOES PACKED IN OIL
- ½ CUP PISTACHIOS, SHELLED
- ½ CUP ITALIAN PARSLEY, CHOPPED
- 1 TEASPOON FRESH THYME, MINCED
- ZEST AND JUICE FROM ½ LEMON
- 1 TEASPOON SEA SALT
- 1 TEASPOON FRESHLY GROUND BLACK PEPPER

DIRECTIONS

1. Place the 1 tablespoon of olive oil in a saute pan and warm over medium heat. Add shallot and cook until light brown, about 3 to 5 minutes.

2. Deglaze pan with vermouth. Remove from heat and let cool.

3. Place all ingredients into a food processor and puree until well combined. If too thick, add water 1 teaspoon at a time until the desired consistency.

Whipped Herb Butter

YIELD: ½ **CUP**

ACTIVE TIME: **10 MINUTES**

TOTAL TIME: **10 MINUTES**

Chances are you've been blown away by an herb butter at a fancy restaurant. This recipe brings it well within your reach.

INGREDIENTS

1 TABLESPOON EXTRA
    VIRGIN OLIVE OIL

1 GARLIC CLOVE

1 TABLESPOON THYME, CHOPPED

1 TABLESPOON BASIL, CHOPPED

1 STICK OF BUTTER

DIRECTIONS

1. Place the olive oil and garlic in a food processor and puree until the garlic is finely chopped. Add the thyme and basil and blend until the herbs have colored the oil.

2. Using the whisk attachment on your hand-mixer, place the butter in the work bowl and whip at medium speed until it softens and lightens in color, about 5 minutes.

3. Add the herb oil to the butter and beat for 1 minute, or until combined.

4. Remove butter and place in the refrigerator until ready to serve.

Venice Beach Wines Classic Hummus

YIELD: **6 CUPS**

ACTIVE TIME: **5 MINUTES**

TOTAL TIME: **5 MINUTES**

Venice Beach Wines is a great place to unwind. Try this intriguing hummus and you'll start to understand why.

INGREDIENTS

4 CUPS CHICKPEAS

2 CUPS OF EDAMAME

½ CUP WATER

¾ CUP EXTRA VIRGIN OLIVE OIL, PLUS MORE FOR GARNISH

2 TABLESPOONS SALT

2 TABLESPOONS TAHINI

3 GARLIC CLOVES

TOASTED PINE NUTS, FOR GARNISH

DIRECTIONS

1. Place all ingredients in a blender and puree until smooth.

2. To serve, drizzle with extra virgin olive oil and top with toasted pine nuts.

Simon's Market Yogurt Dip

YIELD: **1 CUP**

ACTIVE TIME: **5 MINUTES**

TOTAL TIME: **5 MINUTES**

Artichokes, grilled cabbage, and anything savory is a good match for this tangy dip.

INGREDIENTS

1 CUP PLAIN YOGURT

2 TABLESPOONS CUMIN

BLACK PEPPER, TO TASTE

JUICE OF 2 LEMONS

3 TABLESPOONS OLIVE OIL

2 DILL SPRIGS, CHOPPED

DIRECTIONS

1. Place all ingredients in a bowl and stir until well combined. Refrigerate until ready to serve.

Strawberry Salsa

YIELD: **2 CUPS**

ACTIVE TIME: **5 MINUTES**

TOTAL TIME: **5 MINUTES**

Strawberries in salsa?
Don't knock it till you've tried it.

INGREDIENTS

1 PINT STRAWBERRIES, DICED

½ CUP FRESH CILANTRO, CHOPPED

¼ CUP FRESH MINT, CHOPPED

1 SHALLOT, MINCED

½ ENGLISH CUCUMBER, DICED

1 JALAPEÑO PEPPER, MINCED

DIRECTIONS

1. Place all ingredients in a bowl and stir until combined. Serve immediately.

Mike's Hot Honey Mustard Dip

YIELD: **½ CUP**

ACTIVE TIME: **2 MINUTES**

TOTAL TIME: **2 MINUTES**

This specialty honey used to be tough to track down, but is increasingly available across the country.

INGREDIENTS

½ CUP MAYONNAISE

2 TABLESPOONS DIJON MUSTARD

2 TABLESPOONS MIKE'S HOT HONEY

1 TABLESPOON LEMON JUICE

SALT, TO TASTE

DIRECTIONS

1. Place all of the ingredients in a bowl and stir to combine. Season with salt and serve immediately.

Chipotle and Adobo Crema

YIELD: **1 CUP**

ACTIVE TIME: **3 MINUTES**

TOTAL TIME: **3 MINUTES**

Serve this smoky sauce with crudité for a burst of flavor. Be warned: this sauce is addictive.

INGREDIENTS

8 OZ. PLAIN GREEK YOGURT

1 TABLESPOON DIJON MUSTARD

1 TABLESPOON ADOBO SAUCE

1 CHIPOTLE IN ADOBO, MINCED,
   PLUS MORE TO TASTE

1 TABLESPOON HONEY,
   PLUS MORE TO TASTE

DIRECTIONS

1. Place all ingredients in a bowl and stir until well combined. Add additional honey and chipotle to taste.

2. Serve with pita chips, crudité, and charcuterie.

Black Bean Hummus

YIELD: **4 CUPS**

ACTIVE TIME: **10 MINUTES**

TOTAL TIME: **10 MINUTES**

Don't trust the subdued appearance of this hummus, as it's exploding with flavor.

INGREDIENTS

2 (15 OZ.) CANS BLACK BEANS

¼ CUP TAHINI

¾ CUP FRESH LIME JUICE

¾ CUP EXTRA VIRGIN OLIVE OIL

2 TEASPOONS SEA SALT

1 TABLESPOON FRESHLY
   GROUND BLACK PEPPER

1 TEASPOON TABASCO™

1 TEASPOON ANCHOVY PASTE

CILANTRO LEAVES, CHOPPED,
   FOR GARNISH

DIRECTIONS

1. Place all ingredients in a food processor and blend until desired consistency. If too thick, add a tablespoon of water. If too thin, add more black beans.

2. Garnish with cilantro and serve with warm pita triangles and crudité.

Sunchoke Aioli

YIELD: ½ **CUP**
ACTIVE TIME: **10 MINUTES**
TOTAL TIME: **35 MINUTES**

The nutty, slightly savory flavor of sunchokes gets showcased perfectly in this spread.

INGREDIENTS

2 SUNCHOKES

2 EGG YOLKS

½ GARLIC CLOVE, MINCED

½ TEASPOON DIJON MUSTARD

1 TEASPOON LEMON JUICE

½ CUP EXTRA VIRGIN OLIVE OIL

SALT AND PEPPER, TO TASTE

DIRECTIONS

1. In a small saucepan, add the sunchokes and cover with water.

2. Boil for 20 to 25 minutes, or until the interior flesh is very tender.

3. Remove from boiling water and submerge in ice water. Remove, cut sunchokes in half, and remove meat with a spoon.

4. Mash the sunchoke meat with a fork. Add the egg yolks, garlic, mustard, and lemon juice and whisk vigorously until the mixture is nice and smooth.

5. Slowly drizzle in the oil, whisking constantly. Season with salt and pepper and serve.

Chicken Skin Butter

YIELD: **½ CUP**

ACTIVE TIME: **15 MINUTES**

TOTAL TIME: **30 MINUTES**

Once you try this butter you're certain to think up 100 pairings to go with it.

INGREDIENTS

SKIN FROM 2 LARGE
 CHICKEN THIGHS

FLAKY SEA SALT, TO TASTE

½ CUP BUTTER, SOFTENED

½ TEASPOON CHIVES, CHOPPED

DIRECTIONS

1. Preheat the oven to 400°F.

2. Lay the chicken skin on a cutting board, skin side down, and use a small, sharp knife to scrape off any excess fat and meat.

3. Stretch the skins out on a parchment-lined baking sheet and sprinkle with flaky sea salt.

4. Lay a second sheet of parchment paper over the skins and place a second baking sheet on top. Place both trays in the oven for 10 minutes, until the skins are golden and crisp. Remove and let the skins cool.

5. Once cooled, chop the skin into small, fine pieces. Add the butter and skin to a bowl and whisk until combined. Fold in the chives and serve.

Lady & Larder Bay Blue Green Goddess Crudité Dip

YIELD: **6 CUPS**

ACTIVE TIME: **5 MINUTES**

TOTAL TIME: **5 MINUTES**

One of Lady & Larder's most popular offerings, they were kind enough to provide us with the recipe for this rich, zesty dip.

INGREDIENTS

1 ½ CUPS MAYONNAISE

2 CUPS SOUR CREAM

1 6-OZ. WEDGE POINT
REYES BAY BLUE CHEESE

1 TABLESPOON PARSLEY, CHOPPED

1 TABLESPOON TARRAGON,
CHOPPED

1 TABLESPOON CHIVES, CHOPPED

1 TABLESPOON BASIL, CHOPPED

1 TABLESPOON RED WINE VINEGAR

1 TABLESPOON SUGAR

1 TEASPOON GARLIC POWDER

1 TABLESPOON WORCESTERSHIRE
SAUCE

CRACKED PEPPER AND
KOSHER SALT, TO TASTE

DIRECTIONS

1. Combine all ingredients in a food processor except for the blue cheese. Add blue cheese and take care not to overmix to maintain the chunky texture. Refrigerate until ready to serve.

Raita

YIELD: ½ TO ¾ CUP

ACTIVE TIME: **5 MINUTES**

TOTAL TIME: **5 MINUTES**

This refreshing Indian specialty can help balance some of the spicier spreads on your board.

INGREDIENTS

½ CUP PLAIN YOGURT

½ ENGLISH CUCUMBER, SEEDED AND DICED

¼ CUP FRESH CILANTRO, CHOPPED

2 SCALLIONS, MINCED

¼ TEASPOON CORIANDER

½ TEASPOON SEA SALT

½ TEASPOON FRESHLY GROUND BLACK PEPPER

DIRECTIONS

1. Place all ingredients in a bowl and stir until well combined. Refrigerate for 1 hour before serving.

Peanut Satay Dip

YIELD: **1 CUP**

ACTIVE TIME: **10 MINUTES**

TOTAL TIME: **10 MINUTES**

This tangy, salty dip is perfect for any board loaded with savory options, and pairs particularly well with Crispy Wonton Skins (see page 47).

INGREDIENTS

1 CUP CREAMY PEANUT BUTTER

2 TABLESPOONS RICE WINE VINEGAR

¼ CUP SOY SAUCE

1 TABLESPOON HONEY

¼ CUP BOILING WATER

JUICE OF 2 LIMES

1 TEASPOON RED CHILI SAUCE

1 TEASPOON FRESHLY GROUND BLACK PEPPER

DIRECTIONS

1. Combine all ingredients in a bowl. Mix until well combined. Serve warm.

Rustic Bakery Fava Bean Spread

YIELD: **4 CUPS**

ACTIVE TIME: **20 MINUTES**

TOTAL TIME: **35 MINUTES**

This spread is packed with vitamins and flavor, so don't be scared off by the need to shell the fava beans.

INGREDIENTS

4 CUPS FAVA BEANS IN THE SHELL

½ TO 1 CUP OLIVE OIL

15 GARLIC CLOVES

5 TABLESPOONS ROSEMARY, CHOPPED

½ CUP WATER

SALT AND PEPPER, TO TASTE

DIRECTIONS

1. Bring water to boil in a medium saucepan. Shell the fava beans, add them to the saucepan, and cook for 1 to 2 minutes. Submerge in cold water and then remove the skins.

2. Heat ½ cup of oil in a large skillet over low heat. Add the fava beans and cook, while stirring, until tender. Set the beans aside.

3. In the same pan, add the garlic and cook until golden, adding oil as needed. Add rosemary and cook while stirring for 2 minutes, or until fragrant.

4. Working in four batches, place ingredients in a food processor and puree until smooth. Make sure not to overprocess.

5. Season to taste and serve.

Traditional Hummus

YIELD: **1 1/3 CUPS**

ACTIVE TIME: **15 MINUTES**

TOTAL TIME: **15 MINUTES**

Relying on store-bought varieties of hummus can sink a whole serving board. Luckily, this version is here to save the day.

INGREDIENTS

1 (15 OZ.) CAN CHICKPEAS
    OR 2 CUPS DRAINED,
    COOKED CHICKPEAS

3 TABLESPOONS EXTRA
    VIRGIN OLIVE OIL

3 TABLESPOONS TAHINI

1 ½ TABLESPOONS LEMON JUICE,
    PLUS MORE AS NEEDED

1 SMALL GARLIC CLOVE,
    ROUGHLY CHOPPED

1 TEASPOON SALT

½ TEASPOON FINELY
    GROUND BLACK PEPPER

DIRECTIONS

1. If using canned chickpeas, drain the chickpeas into a strainer, reserving the liquid from the can. If time allows, remove the skins from each of the chickpeas. This will make your hummus much smoother.

2. Place the chickpeas, olive oil, tahini, lemon juice, garlic, salt, and pepper in a food processor.

3. Puree hummus until it is very smooth, about 5 to 10 minutes. Scrape down the sides of the bowl as needed to integrate any large chunks.

4. Taste and adjust seasonings to taste. If your hummus is stiffer than you'd like, add 2 to 3 tablespoons of the reserved chickpea liquid and blend until desired consistency is achieved.

5. Scrape the hummus into a bowl and serve with pita or vegetables.

HUMMUS VARIATIONS: For even tastier and more authentic hummus, soak dried chickpeas overnight and cook them for 1 hour. You can also dress it up with any of the following options:

1. *Add 1 to 3 teaspoons of spices like cumin, sumac, harissa, or smoked paprika.*

2. *Drizzle a little pomegranate molasses on top.*

3. *For a roasted vegetable hummus, blend in 1 cup of roasted eggplant, zucchini, bell peppers, or garlic.*

4. *For an olive hummus, fold in ¾ cup of chopped green or black olives.*

5. *For a nutty hummus, blend in some lightly toasted walnuts, almonds, or pine nuts.*

6. *For a lemony hummus, add ¼ cup of chopped preserved lemons.*

Roasted Beet Spread

YIELD: 2 CUPS

ACTIVE TIME: **20 MINUTES**

TOTAL TIME: **1 HOUR AND 30 MINUTES**

Roasting brings the best out of beets. The combination of this spread and goat cheese can't be beet.

INGREDIENTS

4 BEETS, PEELED AND CUBED

¼ CUP EXTRA VIRGIN OLIVE OIL

½ TEASPOON SEA SALT,
   PLUS MORE TO TASTE

¾ TEASPOON CUMIN SEEDS

¾ TEASPOON CORIANDER SEEDS

2 TEASPOONS MINCED GARLIC
   (ABOUT 2 CLOVES), PLUS MORE
   TO TASTE

2 TEASPOONS GREEN CHILI,
   RIBBED, SEEDED, AND MINCED,
   PLUS MORE TO TASTE

2 TEASPOONS FRESH LEMON JUICE,
   PLUS MORE TO TASTE

⅓ CUP CILANTRO LEAVES, MINCED

DIRECTIONS

1. Preheat the oven to 400°F.

2. Line a baking sheet with parchment paper. Place the beets in a bowl with 2 tablespoons of the olive oil and ¼ teaspoon of the salt. Toss to coat.

3. Arrange the beets on the baking sheet in a single layer and roast for about 1 hour, tossing periodically, until the beets are tender. You should have about 2 cups.

4. Heat the cumin and coriander seeds in a dry skillet over medium-high heat for about 2 minutes, stirring constantly, until they release their fragrance and change color slightly. Be careful not to burn them or they will become bitter.

5. Grind the seeds in a spice grinder or crush with a mortar and pestle.

6. Place the beets into a high-speed blender or food processor and add the remaining olive oil and salt, the ground seeds, garlic, chili, and lemon juice. Puree until well combined.

7. Adjust the garlic, chili, lemon juice, and salt to taste. Transfer the dip to a bowl, stir in the cilantro, and serve.

Taramasalata

YIELD: **1 TO 1 ½ CUPS**

ACTIVE TIME: **10 MINUTES**

TOTAL TIME: **10 MINUTES**

A rich and salty Greek classic that will transport you to the shores of the Aegean. It will go well with the Sea Salt and Herb Crackers on page 41.

INGREDIENTS

10 SLICES STALE WHITE BREAD, CRUSTS REMOVED

4 OZ. FISH ROE

JUICE OF 2 LEMONS

1 SMALL RED ONION, GRATED

¾ CUP EXTRA VIRGIN OLIVE OIL

OLIVES, FOR GARNISH

PARSLEY, FOR GARNISH

DIRECTIONS

1. Soak bread in water, then squeeze out excess water. Place all ingredients except oil in a food processor. Puree until smooth, gradually adding the oil until the desired texture is achieved.

2. Place in a serving dish and chill for 2 to 3 hours. Garnish with olives and parsley and serve with pita and vegetables.

White Bean and Rosemary Spread

YIELD: **2 CUPS**

ACTIVE TIME: **10 MINUTES**

TOTAL TIME: **45 MINUTES**

Once you procure some fresh rosemary, this spread can be made from ingredients that are always on hand.

INGREDIENTS

2 CUPS COOKED WHITE BEANS OR 1 (15 OZ.) CAN OF WHITE BEANS, RINSED AND DRAINED

2 TABLESPOONS OLIVE OIL

2 TEASPOONS BALSAMIC VINEGAR

2 GARLIC CLOVES, MINCED

1 TABLESPOON ROSEMARY, MINCED

⅓ CUP CELERY, MINCED

SALT AND FRESHLY GROUND BLACK PEPPER, TO TASTE

2 PINCHES OF RED PEPPER FLAKES (OPTIONAL)

DIRECTIONS

1. Place the beans in a bowl, and mash about half of them with a fork. Add the olive oil, vinegar, garlic, rosemary, and celery and toss well.

2. Season with salt, pepper, and red pepper flakes, if desired.

3. Cover. Let stand for about 30 minutes and season to taste before serving. If refrigerated, allow to come to room temperature before serving.

Rustic Bakery Chickpea Spread

YIELD: **4 CUPS**

ACTIVE TIME: **10 MINUTES**

TOTAL TIME: **10 MINUTES**

The addition of cilantro separates this spread from a traditional hummus.

INGREDIENTS

2 GARLIC CLOVES

½ BUNCH CILANTRO, STEMS REMOVED

1 (15 OZ.) CAN OF CHICKPEAS, RINSED AND DRAINED

ZEST AND JUICE OF 2 LEMONS

¾ CUP TAHINI

4 TABLESPOONS WATER, PLUS MORE AS NEEDED

4 TABLESPOONS OLIVE OIL

2 TEASPOONS SALT

½ TEASPOON PEPPER

DIRECTIONS

1. Mince the garlic in a food processor.

2. Add the cilantro and pulse until combined.

3. Add the remaining ingredients and puree until smooth. Add additional water as needed to reach the desired consistency.

Roasted Pumpkin Dip

YIELD: **2 CUPS**

ACTIVE TIME: **5 MINUTES**

TOTAL TIME: **35 MINUTES**

Pumpkins are king once the weather gets cold. Their sweet, savory flavor is reminiscent of a warm fire on a crisp fall day.

INGREDIENTS

1 MEDIUM SUGAR PUMPKIN

1 TABLESPOON VEGETABLE OIL

2 TEASPOONS SEA SALT

1 TEASPOON FRESHLY
    GROUND BLACK PEPPER

¼ CUP EXTRA VIRGIN OLIVE OIL

1 TEASPOON FRESH THYME

¼ TEASPOON FRESHLY
    GROUND NUTMEG

¼ CUP PARMESAN CHEESE, GRATED

1 TABLESPOON LEMON JUICE

1 TABLESPOON PLAIN GREEK
    YOGURT OR SOUR CREAM

DIRECTIONS

1. Preheat the oven to 425°F. Cut the pumpkin in half, discard the seeds, brush it with the vegetable oil, and sprinkle with 1 teaspoon of the salt. Place on a baking sheet and bake for 25 to 30 minutes. Remove and let cool.

2. Scrape insides from the pumpkin and place in a food processor. Add the remaining ingredients and blend until smooth. Serve immediately.

PRO TIP: Substituting roasted butternut squash for the pumpkin is another option you can utilize in the fall.

Green Hummus

YIELD: **1 1/3 CUPS**

ACTIVE TIME: **10 MINUTES**

TOTAL TIME: **10 MINUTES**

Acquiring its vivid green color from an array of fresh herbs, this hummus brightens up any serving board.

INGREDIENTS

¼ CUP TAHINI

¼ CUP FRESH LEMON JUICE
(1 LARGE LEMON)

2 TABLESPOONS OLIVE OIL,
PLUS MORE FOR SERVING

¼ CUP PARSLEY, CHOPPED

¼ CUP CILANTRO, CHOPPED

2 JALAPEÑO PEPPERS, SEEDED,
STEMMED, AND CHOPPED

3 GREEN ONIONS, CHOPPED,
PLUS MORE FOR GARNISH

2 GARLIC CLOVES, MINCED

½ TEASPOON SALT, PLUS
MORE TO TASTE

1 (15 OZ.) CAN OF CHICKPEAS,
DRAINED AND RINSED

1 TO 2 TABLESPOONS WATER
(AS NEEDED)

FRESH HERBS, CHOPPED,
FOR GARNISH (OPTIONAL)

DIRECTIONS

1. Add the tahini and lemon juice to a food processor and puree for about 1 minute. Use a plastic spatula to scrape down the sides of the bowl if needed.

2. Add olive oil, parsley, cilantro, jalapeños, green onion, garlic, and salt. Puree for about 1 minute, scraping down the bowl as necessary.

3. Add the chickpeas and puree until the hummus has a thick and smooth texture, about 1 to 2 minutes. Scrape down the bowl a few times while pureeing.

4. If hummus is too thick, puree and slowly add 1 to 2 tablespoons water until it reaches the desired consistency.

5. Transfer the hummus into a small serving bowl. Drizzle a tablespoon of olive oil on top and garnish with the additional green onions and herbs, if using.

6. Serve or store in an airtight container and refrigerate for up to 1 week.

Trout Pâté

YIELD: **4 CUPS**

ACTIVE TIME: **10 MINUTES**

TOTAL TIME: **10 MINUTES**

This paté is dynamite on toasted pieces of baguette and crackers.

INGREDIENTS

8 OZ. CREAM CHEESE

8 OZ. CRÈME FRAICHE

1 CUP SHALLOTS, MINCED

1 CUP CHIVES, MINCED

4 OZ. LEMON JUICE

3 TEASPOONS KOSHER SALT

2 ¼ CUPS SMOKED TROUT

DIRECTIONS

1. Place the cream cheese and crème fraiche into the bowl of a standing mixer and turn on low. Mix until combined.

2. Add the shallots, chives, lemon juice, and salt. Continue to mix on low.

3. Add smoked trout and increase speed until the meat is shredded but not pulverized.

4. Scoop from mixing bowl and serve.

Baba Ganoush

YIELD: **2 CUPS**

ACTIVE TIME: **25 MINUTES**

TOTAL TIME: **45 MINUTES**

Roasting the eggplants is a must for this spread, as it draws out their meaty flavor.

INGREDIENTS

3 MEDIUM EGGPLANTS

½ CUP EXTRA VIRGIN OLIVE OIL

1 TEASPOON SEA SALT

1 TABLESPOON TAHINI

½ TEASPOON CHILI POWDER

JUICE OF 2 LEMONS

1 GARLIC CLOVE, GRATED

1 TEASPOON FRESHLY
    GROUND BLACK PEPPER

DIRECTIONS

1. Preheat oven to 375°F. Cut eggplants in half and poke holes over the surface using a fork. Place in a bowl and toss with 1 to 2 tablespoons of olive oil and the salt. Place the eggplants flesh side up on a baking sheet and bake for 15 to 20 minutes until lightly brown and tender all the way through.

2. Remove eggplant from the oven and allow to cool slightly. Once cool enough to handle, remove skins and discard.

3. Place the eggplant in a food processor with the remaining ingredients and pulse until smooth but textured.

4. Serve immediately or refrigerate until ready to use.

Roasted Artichoke and Garlic Spread

YIELD: **1 CUP**

ACTIVE TIME: **5 MINUTES**

TOTAL TIME: **10 TO 20 MINUTES**

Pairing the nutty flavor of artichokes with the sweetness of roasted garlic makes for an incredibly versatile spread.

INGREDIENTS

1 (12 OZ.) BAG OF FROZEN ARTICHOKE HEARTS, THAWED AND HALVED OR QUARTERED

4 GARLIC CLOVES, PEELED

2 TABLESPOONS WHITE VINEGAR OR APPLE CIDER VINEGAR

¼ TEASPOON SALT

4 TABLESPOONS OLIVE OIL

PINCH OF ONION POWDER (OPTIONAL)

DIRECTIONS

1. Spread the artichoke hearts and garlic on a cookie sheet and broil for 5 to 15 minutes, until browned. Combine all ingredients in a blender or food processor and puree until desired texture is achieved.

2. The spread can be eaten warm immediately or covered and chilled. Serve with bread, use as a sandwich or wrap filling, or use as a dip.

Karla's Guacamole

YIELD: **2 CUPS**

ACTIVE TIME: **10 MINUTES**

TOTAL TIME: **10 MINUTES**

When my sister moved to California, she could reach out the window at her apartment and pluck avocados from a tree. She turned that bit of good fortune into the best guacamole recipe ever.

INGREDIENTS

3 AVOCADOS, HALVED, SEEDED, AND PEELED

JUICE OF 2 TO 3 LIMES, PLUS MORE FOR GARNISH

2 ROMA TOMATOES, SEEDED AND DICED

1 MEDIUM RED ONION, DICED

1 TO 2 CLOVES GARLIC, MINCED

½ TEASPOON SALT

PEPPER, TO TASTE

OLD BAY SEASONING, TO TASTE

1 TABLESPOON CILANTRO, CHOPPED, FOR GARNISH

DIRECTIONS

1. In a large bowl, add the avocados and mash roughly.

2. Coat the avocados with lime juice. Add the tomatoes, onions, garlic, salt, pepper, and Old Bay seasoning.

3. Fold ingredients together until mixture reaches the desired consistency. While a chunkier guacamole is easier for dipping, you can also puree the mixture in a food processor for a smoother finish.

4. Garnish with cilantro. Finish with a final splash of lime juice and serve.

CHAPTER 8

BIGGER BITES

The serving board is a wonderful culinary pasture through which the hungry may graze as they sip drinks, chat, and enjoy the moment. But even the most bountiful collection of little bites will leave some wanting more. Fear not, this chapter proves that the serving board can take on snacks of all sizes, from skewers and tempura to delectable salads.

VENICE
BEACH WINES

NORMA ALVARADO IS A CO-OWNER OF VENICE BEACH WINES
"I am not a chef by trade. Crazily enough, I got involved in this world because Oscar [Hermosillo] and I saw a need in our neighborhood and we wanted a new challenge. We were both social workers, working with people with developmental disabilities. Although we loved our profession, we were still semi-young and were looking to do something creative and fun. In 2006, Oscar and I opened Venice Beach Wines. The first year and a half it was a retail store with wines from all over the world, focusing on small production and eclectic wines, craft beers, and a small selection of quality cheese and charcuterie. Basically, it was a one-stop shop for serving boards. We had jams, mustards, crackers: all the goodies you needed for an amazing meat and cheese platter.

"As we worked on growing the retail business, we also worked on getting the permits to be able to pour wine and be a restaurant. In 2008, we became a wine bar. We are on our 12th year and it's been a crazy, difficult, but wonderful experience. Being in Southern California, we are fortunate to have a large selection of beautiful produce all year long. I love serving boards that have vibrant color, quality ingredients, and fragrant herbs or fruits. I like my boards to be simple, but chic: nothing too fussy or complicated. The first thing I always think about when planning a board is the cheese and charcuterie, but that's because I can eat it every day. I can make a breakfast board that includes eggs, smoked fishes, and pâtés, yummy breads and butter, but I think a board can be almost anything. A few years ago, I served a beautiful Greek-style leg of lamb on a board with roasted vegetables, beautiful herbs, grilled lemons, and garlic for Easter.

"When it comes to my favorite wine or drink to serve along with my boards, I'm a big Rosé fan. There are so many different styles and varietals of Rosé, I think they can easily pair with lots of foods. If I were to have something non-alcoholic, I would make agua fresca using fruits or vegetables that are in season. I particularly love a watermelon-and-mint agua fresca or a cucumber, lemon, and mint."

Venice Beach Wines Curried Couscous

YIELD: **4 CUPS**

ACTIVE TIME: **5 MINUTES**

TOTAL TIME: **20 MINUTES**

The turmeric adds a wonderful color and earthiness, and the lemon omani contributes a heavenly fragrance to this simple couscous dish.

INGREDIENTS

4 CUPS ISRAELI COUSCOUS

1 CUP EXTRA VIRGIN OLIVE OIL

1 ONION, DICED

2 TABLESPOONS CURRY

6 CUPS WATER

1 TEASPOON TURMERIC

SALT, TO TASTE

½ TEASPOON LEMON OMANI
   (DRIED LEMON PEEL, POPULAR
   IN MIDDLE EASTERN CUISINE)

DIRECTIONS

1. Place the couscous in a pan and cook over medium heat. Toast the couscous, stirring constantly. Add the olive oil, onion, curry and turmeric and cook for 5 minutes.

2. Add 4 cups of the water and cook, stirring occasionally, until all of the water has been absorbed.

3. Season with salt to taste. Add 2 cups of water and continue to cook, stirring until the water is absorbed. Stir in lemon omani.

4. Remove from heat and spread on two baking sheets to cool.

Venice Beach Wines Crostini with Ricotta and Pea Tendrils

Topping this crostini with the refreshing flavor of pea tendrils makes it a perfect snack for springtime.

YIELD: **4 TO 6 SERVINGS**

ACTIVE TIME: **15 MINUTES**

TOTAL TIME: **35 MINUTES**

INGREDIENTS

1 BAGUETTE, CUT INTO
   ½-INCH THICK SLICES

7 TABLESPOONS EXTRA
   VIRGIN OLIVE OIL, PLUS
   MORE FOR GARNISH

3 CUPS FRESH WHOLE
   MILK RICOTTA

½ TEASPOON SEA SALT,
   PLUS MORE FOR TOPPING

½ TEASPOON FRESHLY GROUND
   BLACK PEPPER, PLUS MORE
   FOR TOPPING

¼ CUP RAMPS OR GREEN
   GARLIC, BULBS AND STEMS
   ONLY, MINCED

3 TABLESPOONS MINT,
   FINELY CHOPPED

3 TEASPOONS LEMON ZEST

LEMON OLIVE OIL, FOR GARNISH

PEA TENDRILS, FOR GARNISH

DIRECTIONS

1. Preheat oven to 400°F. Lightly brush baguette slices with 1 tablespoon of the olive oil and arrange on baking sheet.

2. Bake in oven for about 12 to 15 minutes, turning the slices over halfway through. When the slices are golden brown on both sides, remove from the oven.

3. Combine ricotta, the remaining olive oil, salt, and pepper in a bowl and stir until the mixture is light and fluffy. Stir in ramps or green garlic, mint, and lemon zest. Spread ricotta on baguette slices.

4. Drizzle lemon olive oil over the crostini. Sprinkle with a few grains of sea salt and black pepper. Top with fresh pea tendrils and serve.

Simon's Market Southern Deviled Eggs

YIELD: **6 EGGS**

ACTIVE TIME: **15 MINUTES**

TOTAL TIME: **30 MINUTES**

Deviled eggs are typically associated with the 1950s, but this version shows that they are a timeless treat.

INGREDIENTS

6 EGGS

2 TABLESPOONS YELLOW MUSTARD

2 TABLESPOONS MAYONNAISE

2 TEASPOONS WHOLE GRAIN MUSTARD

2 CORNICHONS, DICED

2 TEASPOONS PIMENTOS

SALT AND PEPPER, TO TASTE

5 SPRIGS OF PARSLEY, CHOPPED, FOR GARNISH

1 SPRIG OF DILL, FOR GARNISH

1 SLICE OF SPAM, CUT INTO TRIANGLES AND FRIED, FOR GARNISH (OPTIONAL)

DIRECTIONS

1. Hard-boil the eggs and let cool. Remove the yolks.

2. Combine yolks in a small bowl with yellow mustard, mayonnaise, whole grain mustard, cornichons, and pimentos. Season with salt and pepper to taste.

3. Spoon yolk mixture delicately into each egg white shell.

4. Garnish with parsley, dill, and, if using, Spam.

Fontina Jalapeño Hush Puppies

YIELD: **4 TO 6 SERVINGS**

ACTIVE TIME: **15 MINUTES**

TOTAL TIME: **30 MINUTES**

This Southern classic takes a delicious detour through the Southwest thanks to the jalapeño.

INGREDIENTS

2 CUPS VEGETABLE OIL

½ CUP CORNMEAL

3 TABLESPOONS ALL-PURPOSE FLOUR, PLUS 1 ½ TEASPOONS

4 ½ TABLESPOONS SUGAR

¾ TEASPOON SALT

¼ TEASPOON BAKING POWDER

⅛ TEASPOON BAKING SODA

⅛ TEASPOON CAYENNE PEPPER

¼ CUP BUTTERMILK

1 EGG, BEATEN

2 TABLESPOONS JALAPEÑO PEPPER, SEEDED AND CHOPPED

¾ CUP FONTINA CHEESE, GRATED

DIRECTIONS

1. Place oil in a Dutch oven and heat to 320°F.

2. Add the cornmeal, flour, sugar, salt, baking powder, baking soda, and cayenne pepper to a small bowl and whisk until combined.

3. In a separate bowl, add the buttermilk, egg, and jalapeño. Whisk to combine.

4. Combine the buttermilk mixture and the dry mixture.

5. Add the cheese and stir until combined.

6. Drop spoonfuls of the batter into the hot oil and fry until golden brown.

7. Remove from oil with a slotted spoon and place on paper towels to drain.

Tempura Broccoli

YIELD: **4 TO 6 SERVINGS**

ACTIVE TIME: **10 MINUTES**

TOTAL TIME: **20 MINUTES**

Even those who recoil at the thought of broccoli will be unable to turn down this fried version.

INGREDIENTS

1 CUP OIL

4 CUPS WATER

1 TEASPOON SALT, PLUS
   MORE TO TASTE

12 SMALL BROCCOLI FLORETS

¾ CUP ALL-PURPOSE FLOUR

¼ CUP CORNSTARCH

½ TEASPOON BAKING POWDER

1 CUP SODA WATER

BLACK PEPPER, TO TASTE

DIRECTIONS

1. Place the oil in a Dutch oven and heat to 350°F.

2. Place the water and salt in a medium saucepan and bring to a boil. Add the broccoli, cook for 3 minutes, remove and submerge in ice water. Remove and set on a paper towel to dry.

3. Combine ½ cup of the flour, the cornstarch, and the baking powder in a bowl. Pass through a sieve.

4. Add the soda water and whisk until smooth. This is the tempura mix.

5. In a small bowl, add the remaining flour and the broccoli. Mix gently until the broccoli is coated.

6. Dip the pieces of broccoli into the tempura mix. Drop in oil and fry until golden brown.

7. Use a slotted spoon to remove from the oil and set on a paper towel to drain. Season with salt and pepper and serve immediately.

Simon's Market Sardine Salad

YIELD: **4 TO 6 SERVINGS**

ACTIVE TIME: **5 MINUTES**

TOTAL TIME: **5 MINUTES**

Light and packed with protein and flavor, everyone will be walking on air after enjoying this salad.

INGREDIENTS

2 HANDFULS OF WATERCRESS

1 TABLESPOON OLIVE OIL

1 CUP CANNED SARDINES, DRAINED

2 TEASPOONS WHOLE GRAIN MUSTARD

20 CAPERS

1 SQUEEZE OF LEMON JUICE, PLUS MORE TO TASTE

SALT AND PEPPER, TO TASTE

ZEST OF 1 LEMON

LEMON SLICES, FOR GARNISH

DIRECTIONS

1. Place all ingredients, save the lemon slices, in a bowl and toss until combined. Adjust seasoning to taste.

2. Garnish with lemon slices and serve.

Baked Apples Farcie with Calvados, Pork, and Goat Cheese

YIELD: **6 SERVINGS**

ACTIVE TIME: **30 TO 40 MINUTES**

TOTAL TIME: **1 HOUR AND 30 MINUTES**

Inspiration for this recipe struck Stovetopped's Lisa Walker when she came upon a beautifully-worn piece of California oak and a box of apples, along with a creamy wedge of Saint-Maure de Touraine and a half-pound of fresh pork sausage both found in the fridge. Carving the apples requires a little effort and skill that you can manage like a grand-mere. You now have a reason to use that melon-baller shoved at the back of the drawer!

INGREDIENTS

6 PINK LADY APPLES

2 TABLESPOONS OLIVE OIL, PLUS MORE FOR RUBBING

SALT AND BLACK PEPPER, TO TASTE

8 OZ PORK SAUSAGE, CASING REMOVED

4 FRESH SAGE LEAVES

2 SMALL SHALLOTS, DICED

2 TABLESPOONS CALVADOS

2 CUPS GARLIC CROUTONS, CRUSHED (SEE PAGE 214)

2 TABLESPOONS CREAM (OPTIONAL)

1 (2 OZ.) LOG OF GOAT CHEESE, CUT INTO 6 BUTTONS

DIRECTIONS

1. Preheat oven to 350°F. Slice the tops off of the apples and set aside. Use a paring knife to cut a circle in the apples' flesh and then scoop out the center. Make sure to leave a ½-inch thick wall inside the apple.

2. Rub the apples inside and out with olive oil and season all over with salt and pepper. Set aside.

3. In a large skillet, add 2 tablespoons of olive oil and warm over medium-high heat. Crumble the pork sausage into the pan and then add the sage and shallots. Cook for 2 minutes. Splash with Calvados and cook for another 2 minutes until the alcohol has cooked off. Season to taste, remove from heat, and let cool for 10 minutes.

4. In a large mixing bowl, add the croutons, the cooked sausage mixture, and the cooking juices. Add the cream and toss to combine.

5. Fill each apple with 1 teaspoon of the sausage-and-crouton mixture. Next, add the slices of goat cheese. Fill each apple over its brim with the remaining sausage-and-crouton mixture and place in baking dish, careful to balance the top on each apple.

6. Bake for 40 to 45 minutes. Serve hot or warm on a beautiful wooden board with the Fall Salad and Cider Vinaigrette (see page 216).

Garlic Croutons

YIELD: **1 CUP**

ACTIVE TIME: **15 TO 20 MINUTES**

TOTAL TIME: **45 MINUTES**

With this recipe from Chef Lisa Walker, you'll never toss day-old bread in the trash ever again.

INGREDIENTS

3 SLICES OF DAY-OLD BAGUETTE

¼ CUP OLIVE OIL

1 GARLIC CLOVE, MINCED

KOSHER SALT AND BLACK PEPPER, TO TASTE

DIRECTIONS

1. Preheat the oven to 400°F.

2. Place the slices of bread on a baking sheet and brush with olive oil. Sprinkle with the garlic, kosher salt, and fresh black pepper.

3. Bake for 15 to 20 minutes until golden brown. Remove, let cool on the pan, and then place in a plastic bag and seal.

4. To make the croutons, crush the bag with the palm of your hand for larger croutons, or roll with a rolling pin for smaller croutons. Store in a plastic bag for up to 4 days or in a freezer for 2 months.

Roasted Shrimp

YIELD: **10 TO 15 SERVINGS**

ACTIVE TIME: **10 MINUTES**

TOTAL TIME: **25 MINUTES**

Tossing shrimp in the oven and crisping them slightly is a clever spin on the classic shrimp cocktail.

INGREDIENTS

2 POUNDS FRESH SHRIMP, SHELLED

3 TABLESPOONS OLIVE OIL

2 TEASPOONS SEA SALT

2 TEASPOONS FRESHLY
GROUND BLACK PEPPER

1 TEASPOON RED PEPPER FLAKES
(OPTIONAL)

DIRECTIONS

1. Preheat oven to 400°F. Place ingredients in a large bowl and toss until the shrimp are evenly coated.

2. In one layer, position the seasoned shrimp on a baking sheet. Bake for 9 to 10 minutes or until slightly browned. Serve warm or at room temperature.

Fall Salad

YIELD: **4 TO 6 SERVINGS**

ACTIVE TIME: **10 MINUTES**

TOTAL TIME: **10 MINUTES**

This lovely salad from Chef Lisa Walker can handle the addition of almost any fruit, nut, or vegetable.

INGREDIENTS

1 HEAD OF BUTTER LETTUCE, WASHED AND SPUN DRY

1 SMALL HEAD OF RADICCHIO, LEAVES PULLED APART

1 HANDFUL OF BABY SPINACH

CIDER VINAIGRETTE (SEE BELOW)

FLAKY SEA SALT, TO TASTE

DIRECTIONS

1. Gently tear the lettuce leaves and radicchio leaves. Add them to a salad bowl with the baby spinach. Leave the baby spinach whole and place the greens in a large salad bowl.

2. Spoon the vinaigrette over the salad greens. Toss gently until all salad greens are evenly dressed. Sprinkle with salt, toss, and serve.

CIDER VINAIGRETTE

INGREDIENTS:

4 TABLESPOONS APPLE CIDER VINEGAR

1 TABLESPOON HONEY

3 TABLESPOONS EXTRA VIRGIN OLIVE OIL

½ TABLESPOON KOSHER SALT

¼ TEASPOON BLACK PEPPER

FLAKY SEA SALT, TO TASTE

DIRECTIONS:

1. Combine the vinegar, honey, extra virgin olive oil, salt, and pepper in a bowl. Whisk to combine, sprinkle with sea salt, and set aside.

Mike's Hot Honey Mustard Pork Skewers

YIELD: **8 SERVINGS**

ACTIVE TIME: **20 MINUTES**

TOTAL TIME: **45 MINUTES**

Looking to spice up your board a little bit?
Give these skewers a try.

INGREDIENTS

¼ CUP DIJON MUSTARD

¼ CUP MIKE'S HOT HONEY

1 TABLESPOON OLIVE OIL

1 ½ POUNDS PORK TENDERLOIN,
     CUT INTO 1-INCH CUBES

8 BAMBOO SKEWERS

2 BELL PEPPERS,
     SEEDED AND CHOPPED

SALT AND PEPPER, TO TASTE

DIRECTIONS

1. Place mustard, honey, and olive oil in a large bowl and stir until smooth. Add pork cubes and toss to coat. Set aside.

2. Soak 8 bamboo skewers in cold water for 20 minutes. Preheat broiler to high and line a broiling pan with foil.

3. Divide pork and peppers into 8 portions and alternate them on the skewers. Season with salt and pepper.

4. Broil or grill for 10 to 15 minutes, turning often until slightly browned and cooked through.

Mike's Hot Honey Cheese-Stuffed Figs with Hot Honey Port Syrup

YIELD: **8 SERVINGS**

ACTIVE TIME: **5 MINUTES**

TOTAL TIME: **15 MINUTES**

Setting some stuffed figs out means that your gathering is at a high level. Drizzling them with a spicy, rich syrup places it in rarefied air.

INGREDIENTS

⅓ CUP PORT

4 TABLESPOONS MIKE'S HOT HONEY

8 FRESH FIGS

8 TABLESPOONS CREAM CHEESE AT ROOM TEMPERATURE

DIRECTIONS

1. In a small saucepan, add the Port and honey and cook over low to medium heat. Bring to a simmer and cook until the consistency becomes thick, about 3 to 5 minutes.

2. Remove from heat and let cool. Cut the stem off of each fig. Then cut each fig crosswise and open.

3. Place a teaspoon of cream cheese in the center of each fig and drizzle with honey port syrup.

SIMON'S
MARKET

WHEN SIMON'S MARKET OPENED ITS FIRST store on Rose Avenue in Venice, California, it became the neighborhood go-to for impromptu party supplies. Carrying a well-curated section of wine and beer, along with all kinds of specialty items that work perfectly on a board, their loyal clientele started to ask if they could make cheese and charcuterie boards to-go. Joshua Montoya started crafting boards for the neighborhood, and the business grew. Now he incorporates many of his own recipes into his premade boards, suggests wine and beer pairings, and continues to add to the ever-growing stock of local and artisan-made products sold at his store.

Murray's Cheese Dill Pickle Arancini

YIELD: **8 TO 10 SERVINGS**

ACTIVE TIME: **30 MINUTES**

TOTAL TIME: **1 HOUR AND 30 MINUTES**

It's not easy to outshine a fried, golden coating, but the multifaceted flavor of dill somehow manages to do just that in this dish.

INGREDIENTS

FOR CAJUN REMOULADE:

1 CUP MAYONNAISE

2 TABLESPOONS DIJON MUSTARD

1 TEASPOON HOT SAUCE

2 TEASPOONS CAJUN SEASONING

1 LEMON, ZESTED AND JUICED

1 GARLIC CLOVE, MINCED

FOR ARANCINI:

8 CUPS CHICKEN STOCK

1 STICK OF BUTTER

2 CUPS ARBORIO RICE

1 SMALL WHITE ONION, MINCED

1 CUP WHITE WINE

1 ½ CUPS HAVARTI
    WITH DILL, GRATED

1 ½ CUPS CRISP & CO. GRAND
    DILL PICKLES, CHOPPED

SALT AND PEPPER, TO TASTE

4 CUPS CANOLA OR
    VEGETABLE OIL

6 LARGE EGGS, BEATEN

5 CUPS PANKO BREAD CRUMBS

DIRECTIONS

1. To make Cajun remoulade, combine all ingredients in a medium bowl, then refrigerate until ready to serve.

2. To make the arancini, heat the chicken stock in a pot until simmering. In a separate pot, melt the butter over high heat.

3. Once the butter is bubbling, add the rice and the onion and cook until the onion become translucent, about 4 minutes.

4. Deglaze the pot with the white wine and reduce until the wine has almost completely evaporated. Then, reduce the heat to medium-high and begin adding the hot chicken stock ¼ cup at a time, stirring frequently until incorporated and reduced slightly. Continue this process until all the liquid has been added and the rice is cooked.

5. Turn off the heat and add the cheese and pickles, seasoning with salt and pepper to taste. Pour the mixture onto a sheet tray and let cool.

6. Meanwhile, place the oil in a large pot and cook over medium heat until it reaches 350°F.

7. Once the risotto mixture is cool, form into golf ball-sized spheres. Submerge in the eggs, then coat with the bread crumbs.

8. Place the balls in the oil and cook until warmed through and golden brown on the outside.

9. Serve with Cajun remoulade.

Blue Cheese Fritters

YIELD: **4 TO 6 SERVINGS**

ACTIVE TIME: **15 MINUTES**

TOTAL TIME: **30 MINUTES**

Using Cashel blue adds a touch of class to what is traditionally thought of as pub food.

INGREDIENTS

2 CUPS OIL

3 EGGS

¼ CUP ALL-PURPOSE FLOUR

1 CUP PANKO BREAD CRUMBS,
   REDUCED TO A FINE POWDER
   IN A FOOD PROCESSOR

6 OZ. CASHEL BLUE,
   ROLLED INTO 12 BALLS OR
   CUT INTO 12 CUBES

SALT, TO TASTE

DIRECTIONS

1. Place the oil in a medium saucepan and heat to 350°F.

2. Place the eggs in a bowl and beat with a fork. Place the flour and bread crumbs in separate bowls.

3. Dredge the balls of cheese in the flour, remove, and shake to remove excess flour. Place the floured blue cheese in the egg wash and coat evenly. Remove from egg wash, shake to remove excess egg, and gently coat with bread crumbs.

4. Place the balls in the hot oil and fry until golden brown. Use a slotted spoon to remove from the oil. Set on paper towels to drain and season with salt. Allow to cool slightly before serving.

Corn Beignets

YIELD: **4 TO 6 SERVINGS**

ACTIVE TIME: **10 MINUTES**

TOTAL TIME: **30 MINUTES**

The corn kernels add a wonderful texture to these pillowy, fried balls of dough.

INGREDIENTS

¼ CUP MILK

⅛ TEASPOON SALT

2 TABLESPOONS BUTTER

¼ CUP FLOUR

1 EGG

¼ CUP CORN

½ TEASPOON CILANTRO, CHOPPED

2 CUPS OIL

DIRECTIONS

1. In a medium saucepan, add milk, salt, and butter. Bring to a boil.

2. Add the flour and stir constantly until a ball of dough forms.

3. Remove the pan from heat. Let the dough cool for 10 minutes.

4. Add the egg to the pan and whisk vigorously.

5. Once the egg is combined, add the corn and cilantro. Stir until combined.

6. Place the oil in a Dutch oven and heat to 350°F.

7. Spoon small amounts of batter into the hot oil and cook until golden brown.

8. Remove with a slotted spoon and set on a paper towel to drain. Serve when cool enough to handle.

Artisanal Cheese Ball

YIELD: **1 CHEESE BALL**

ACTIVE TIME: **15 MINUTES**

TOTAL TIME: **1 HOUR AND 30 MINUTES**

This artisan cheese ball recipe is a stand-alone hit on any board and a great textural diversion on a larger spread. To make it vegetarian, substitute smoked almonds for the bacon.

INGREDIENTS

6 OZ. FROMAGE BLANC

3 OZ. FINELY SHREDDED
    AGED CHEDDAR

3 OZ. CRUMBLED BLUE CHEESE

½ TABLESPOON SOUR CREAM

1 OR 2 DASHES
    WORCESTERSHIRE SAUCE

¼ TEASPOON GARLIC POWDER

¼ TEASPOON FRESH
    CRACKED BLACK PEPPER

⅛ TEASPOON SALT

2 GREEN ONIONS, THINLY SLICED

1 CUP BACON, MINCED

DIRECTIONS

1. Combine the cheeses, sour cream, Worcestershire sauce, garlic powder, pepper, and salt in a food processor or the bowl of a standing mixer. Puree or beat on low for 3 minutes or until mixture is smooth.

2. Fold in the green onions, place mixture in a large bowl, and shape into a ball with a large mixing spoon. Chill for at least 1 hour.

3. Meanwhile, cook bacon in a skillet over medium heat for about 6 minutes until crisp. Drain on paper towels.

4. Dice or crumble and set aside.

5. Gently remove cheese ball from bowl and spread bacon bits on wax paper or cutting board. Roll the cheese ball until evenly coated.

6. Serve at room temperature with assorted crackers.

HAYDEN WINE BAR

CHEF ARI KOLENDER OF HAYDEN WINE BAR, a James Beard nominee, recently moved to Los Angeles and opened his casual eatery near the train stop in Culver City. Hoping to cater to neighborhood locals and commuters alike, he has a passion for seafood and often adds tinned fish from around the world to his creations for a surprising and tasty twist on any board.

"A board should consist of just enough ingredients to give it range and purpose," says Kolender. "Two cheeses, one soft, one hard. Personally, I love an aged Comte and Sofia Capriole goat cheese. One nice salami, such as Saucisson Sec Olives, salted Marcona Almonds, honey dates, fresh country bread, and a secret weapon. I love to incorporate tinned fish from Spain and Portugal. These are world class and should not be taken for granted! Jose Gourmet and La Brújula are two great purveyors that are easy to obtain in the states.

"Another form of fish that works perfectly is a smoked trout dip. I love to pair fresh and pickled veggies with these fish and serve with Sauce Gribiche, which is a French fancy egg salad. I adore radishes with salted butter from Normandy, pickled red onions, pickled Japanese turnips, and sweet peppers.

Gribiche

YIELD: **5 CUPS**

ACTIVE TIME: **5 MINUTES**

TOTAL TIME: **5 MINUTES**

Don't be put off by the foreign name: this dish is easy to make and can be thrown together in a hurry.

INGREDIENTS

11 EGGS, HARDBOILED

6 TABLESPOONS MUSTARD

6 TABLESPOONS LEMON JUICE

4 TABLESPOONS CAPERS, CHOPPED

2 TEASPOONS SALT

2 TABLESPOONS WHITE PEPPER

1 CUP OLIVE OIL

2 TEASPOONS PARSLEY, CHIFFONADE

½ TEASPOON TARRAGON, MINCED

½ TEASPOON CHERVIL, MINCED

3 TABLESPOONS CHIVES, MINCED

DIRECTIONS

1. Separate the egg whites and yolks of the hardboiled eggs. Place the yolks into a bowl. Chop the whites and reserve.

2. Add the mustard, lemon juice, capers, salt, and pepper into the bowl containing the yolks.

3. Using a whisk, mash the yolks until completely disbursed. Then slowly whisk in the olive oil.

4. Once mixed, add the egg whites and the herbs. Stir until fully incorporated and serve.

Pickled Turnips

YIELD: **4 SERVINGS**

ACTIVE TIME: **10 MINUTES**

TOTAL TIME: **12 HOURS**

Turnip is the pickle of choice in the Middle East. Take a cue from them and put these alongside any Middle Eastern or Mediterranean foods that make it onto your boards.

INGREDIENTS

1 JAPANESE TURNIP

4 CUPS RICE WINE VINEGAR

2 CUPS WATER

½ CUP FISH SAUCE

1 ¼ CUPS SUGAR

¼ CUP LIME JUICE

DIRECTIONS

1. Remove the stem from the turnip and run the bulb under cold water until clean. Cut into even quarters, then place into a container that can take on heated liquid.

2. Place the remaining ingredients into a small pot. Bring the contents of the pot to a steady boil and then pour over the turnips.

3. Cover the container with an airtight lid and allow to cool to room temperature. Once cooled, store in the refrigerator overnight before serving.

CHAPTER 9:

DESSERTS

---

*If your sweet tooth is craving some attention
after so much savory goodness the recipes
in this chapter not only make for excellent
after-dinner treats, they also lend themselves
to being presented on serving boards. And
remember, if you use cast-iron, once the pan
has cooled down, you can just set it on the
table and let everyone help themselves.*

Honey Roasted Figs

YIELD: **4 SERVINGS**

ACTIVE TIME: **5 MINUTES**

TOTAL TIME: **10 MINUTES**

The honey and cinnamon accentuate the sweetness and nuttiness that the fig is famous for while the goat cheese adds a luxurious creaminess.

INGREDIENTS

2 TABLESPOONS HONEY

4 BLACK MISSION FIGS, HALVED

⅛ TEASPOON CINNAMON

GOAT CHEESE, CRUMBLED, TO TASTE

DIRECTIONS

1. In a medium nonstick sauté pan, add the honey and warm over medium heat.

2. Place the cut figs facedown and cook for 5 minutes, or until golden brown.

3. Sprinkle the cinnamon over the figs and gently stir to coat. Remove figs from the pan and serve.

Venice Beach Wines Creamy Lemon Curd

YIELD: **4 TO 6 SERVINGS**

ACTIVE TIME: **15 MINUTES**

TOTAL TIME: **25 MINUTES**

This is the perfect palate cleanser after hours of snacking on rich meats and cheeses.

INGREDIENTS

12 LARGE EGG YOLKS

1 ½ CUPS SUGAR

PINCH OF SALT

1 CUP LEMON JUICE

6 TABLESPOONS LEMON ZEST

½ POUND UNSALTED BUTTER, CUT INTO CUBES

12 OZ. CREAM CHEESE, AT ROOM TEMPERATURE

DIRECTIONS

1. In a medium mixing bowl, mix together the egg yolks, sugar, salt, and lemon juice.

2. Place mixture in medium saucepan over low heat.

3. Using a rubber spatula, stir continuously until the mixture begins to thicken. Make sure to maintain a low temperature. Do not boil.

4. Once thickened, remove the pot from the heat and pour the curd through a strainer into a bowl.

5. Add the lemon zest, whisk in the cubed butter until combined, then add the cream cheese and whisk until smooth.

Tiramisu Dip

YIELD: **2 TO 3 CUPS**

ACTIVE TIME: **10 MINUTES**

TOTAL TIME: **10 MINUTES**

Serve this dip with ladyfingers and your fruit of choice for an instant favorite.

INGREDIENTS

1 ⅓ CUPS MASCARPONE CHEESE

½ CUP FRESH RICOTTA CHEESE

½ CUP POWDERED SUGAR

1 TEASPOON PURE
    VANILLA EXTRACT

2 TABLESPOONS BREWED ESPRESSO

1 TEASPOON FINE
    ESPRESSO POWDER

2 TABLESPOONS KAHLUA

1 TEASPOON COCOA POWDER

½ CUP SEMI-SWEET CHOCOLATE
    CHIPS, CHOPPED

DIRECTIONS

1. In a standing mixer, beat together the cheeses, sugar, vanilla, brewed espresso, espresso powder, and Kahlua until thoroughly combined.

2. Place in a serving dish, dust with cocoa powder, and sprinkle with the chocolate chips. Place in refrigerator until chilled. Serve with ladyfingers and fruit of choice.

Brownie Batter Dip

YIELD: **1 TO 1 ½ CUPS**

ACTIVE TIME: **5 MINUTES**

TOTAL TIME: **5 MINUTES**

A perfect complement to the tangy sweetness of strawberries, this dip is chocolate heaven.

INGREDIENTS

8 OZ. CREAM CHEESE OR PLAIN GREEK YOGURT

1 STICK OF BUTTER

1 ½ CUPS POWDERED SUGAR

½ CUP COCOA POWDER

2 TABLESPOONS BROWN SUGAR

⅓ CUP WHOLE MILK

1 TEASPOON VANILLA EXTRACT

½ TEASPOON SEA SALT

DIRECTIONS

1. If using cream cheese, soften it and the butter in microwave for 20 to 30 seconds each, stirring every 5 seconds to achieve the desired consistency.

2. Beat softened cream cheese or yogurt and butter in a bowl until thoroughly combined.

3. Add remaining ingredients and mix until smooth. Serve with fresh strawberries and shortbread.

Chocolate Hazelnut Dip

A homemade version of Nutella, the dip that stole our hearts, this beloved spread brings a hint of umami to any desert board.

YIELD: **1 TO 1 ½ CUPS**

ACTIVE TIME: **15 TO 20 MINUTES**

TOTAL TIME: **30 TO 40 MINUTES**

INGREDIENTS

2 CUPS HAZELNUTS

⅓ CUP SUGAR

1 TEASPOON SEA SALT

16 OZ. SEMI-SWEET
    CHOCOLATE, CHOPPED

1 STICK OF BUTTER

1 CUP HEAVY WHIPPING CREAM

DIRECTIONS

1. Preheat the oven to 350°F. Remove the outer shell from the hazelnuts using a nutcracker.

2. Layer the shelled hazelnuts on a baking sheet in one even layer. Roast in oven for 12 to 15 minutes, then remove and let cool.

3. Place cooled hazelnuts, sugar, and salt into a food processor and blend until the mixture forms a paste.

4. Meanwhile, boil ½ inch of water in a saucepan. Set a bowl over the boiling water, making sure the water does not touch the bowl. This is your double boiler. Add the chocolate to the bowl and allow to melt.

5. Once melted, remove from heat and whisk in butter and cream. Then combine the chocolate mixture and the hazelnut paste.

6. Chill before serving.

Cinnamon Twists

YIELD: **1 TO 1 ½ CUPS**

ACTIVE TIME: **15 TO 20 MINUTES**

TOTAL TIME: **30 MINUTES**

These twists are good enough to serve as the centerpiece of your board. Pair with the Chocolate Hazelnut Dip (see page 245) and you have a combination fit for royalty.

INGREDIENTS

2 SHEETS OF PUFF
PASTRY, THAWED

1 CUP SUGAR

3 ½ TABLESPOONS CINNAMON

1 TEASPOON FRESHLY
GROUND NUTMEG

1 EGG

DIRECTIONS

1. Preheat oven to 375°F. Roll out puff pastry sheets until each is 10 by 12 inches.

2. Combine sugar, cinnamon, and nutmeg in a bowl.

3. Beat the egg in a separate bowl.

4. Lightly brush the tops of each pastry sheet with the egg. Then, sprinkle the sugar-and-spice mixture evenly across the tops of both sheets.

5. Cut the pastries into long strips and twist. Place strips on a baking sheet and bake for 12 to 15 minutes, or until golden brown. Flip each pastry and allow to cook for an additional 2 to 3 minutes.

6. Remove twists from oven and allow to cool until slightly warm. Serve with your favorite dip.

Citrus Rosemary Shortbread

ACTIVE TIME: **20 MINUTES**

TOTAL TIME: **1 HOUR**

YIELD: **2 DOZEN COOKIES**

Serve these simple citrus cookies, flecked with rosemary, on a wooden board with a pot of tea.

INGREDIENTS

2 CUPS BUTTER, SOFTENED

¼ CUP SUGAR

¼ CUP FRESHLY SQUEEZED LEMON JUICE

3 TEASPOONS LEMON ZEST

2 TEASPOONS FRESH ROSEMARY, MINCED

4 ½ CUPS ALL-PURPOSE FLOUR

DEMERARA SUGAR, TO TASTE

DIRECTIONS

1. Preheat oven to 350°F and line a baking sheet with parchment paper.

2. Place all of the ingredients in a mixing bowl, except the flour, and beat at low speed until creamy.

3. Slowly add the flour until the dough is the consistency of coarse crumbs.

4. Press dough into a long cube and chill for 1 hour.

5. Slice the dough into squares, place on the baking sheet, and sprinkle with demerara sugar.

6. Bake for 15 minutes, or until lightly golden brown.

7. Remove from the oven, let cool, and slice into thin wedges.

Chocolate Fondue

ACTIVE TIME: **10 MINUTES**

TOTAL TIME: **20 MINUTES**

YIELD: **4 SERVINGS**

This classic chocolate fondue is easily served on a board with whatever seasonal fruit is available. It pairs particularly well with white peaches.

INGREDIENTS

12 OZ. BITTERSWEET CHOCOLATE, CHOPPED

¾ CUP HEAVY CREAM

1 TEASPOON VANILLA EXTRACT

DIRECTIONS

1. Combine ingredients in a glass bowl.

2. Place the bowl in the microwave and microwave for 2 minutes, or until melted.

3. Stir until smooth and serve immediately.

4. If you want the sauce to remain warm, it can be placed in a traditional fondue pot with a lit burner.

Chocolate Dipped Strawberries

ACTIVE TIME: **20 MINUTES**

TOTAL TIME: **1 HOUR**

YIELD: **1 PINT**

A pile of fresh seasonal strawberries, dipped in either white, milk, or dark chocolate, makes a perfect centerpiece.

INGREDIENTS

1 PINT FRESH STRAWBERRIES, PREFERABLY WITH LONG STEMS

12 OZ. OF WHITE, MILK, OR DARK CHOCOLATE CHIPS

DIRECTIONS

1. Line a baking sheet with parchment or wax paper.

2. Wash and dry strawberries.

3. Pour chocolate chips into a glass bowl and melt in microwave by cooking for about 1 to 2 minutes or until chips are melted completely.

4. While chocolate is hot, dip each strawberry halfway into the melted chocolate.

5. Place on lined baking sheet.

6. When all the strawberries have been dipped, place baking sheet in the refrigerator and chill until the chocolate is set.

Gluten-Free Macaron Bites

ACTIVE TIME: **15 MINUTE**

TOTAL TIME: **45 MINUTES**

YIELD: **8 SERVINGS**

These gooey, sweet, sticky, delicious bites are sure to be an after-dinner favorite.

INGREDIENTS

1 ¼ CUPS SUGAR

4 CUPS UNSWEETENED COCONUT FLAKES

4 EGG WHITES

2 TEASPOONS VANILLA EXTRACT

¼ TEASPOON SALT

DIRECTIONS

1. Preheat oven to 350°F. While preheating, place a cast-iron skillet in the oven to warm up.

2. In a large bowl, combine ingredients.

3. Once the oven has finished heating, remove the skillet. Put the batter into the pan and place back into the oven.

4. Bake for 20 to 30 minutes or until brown on top.

5. Remove the skillet and allow to cool for about 30 minutes. Slice into wedges and serve.

Classic Shortbread Cookie Bars

YIELD: **6 TO 8 SERVINGS**

ACTIVE TIME: **25 MINUTES**

TOTAL TIME: **60 MINUTES**

Perfect for hot summer days with fresh strawberries or cold fall evenings with a cup of coffee, these shortbread cookie bars are good to go all year long.

INGREDIENTS

1 CUP FLOUR

¼ TEASPOON SALT

¼ CUP SUGAR

1 STICK OF UNSALTED BUTTER, CHILLED

½ TEASPOON VANILLA EXTRACT

DIRECTIONS

1. Preheat oven to 300°F. Place a cast-iron skillet in the oven to warm while making the dough.

2. In a large bowl, whisk the flour, salt, and sugar until combined.

3. Cut the chilled butter into slices and add to the flour mixture. Work with your hands until the mixture starts to come together, then add the vanilla extract. Continue to work the mixture until it resembles a coarse meal.

4. Form the dough into a ball, then place on a lightly floured surface and roll out into a circle. The circle should be slightly smaller than the diameter of your skillet, about 8 inches. Slice into 8 wedges.

5. Remove the skillet from the oven and place the wedges into the pan, reforming a circle. Place the skillet back into the oven and bake for 45 minutes or until shortbread is a pale golden color.

6. Remove the skillet and allow to cool for 10 minutes, then serve.

French Apple Tart

This tarte Tatin is a gorgeous dessert that is sure to wow your guests.

ACTIVE TIME: **60 MINUTES**

TOTAL TIME: **2 TO 24 HOURS**

YIELD: **6 TO 8 SERVINGS**

INGREDIENTS

1 CUP FLOUR

½ TEASPOON SALT

1 ½ CUPS SUGAR,
    PLUS 1 TABLESPOON

2 ¾ CUPS BUTTER,
    CUT INTO SMALL PIECES

3 TABLESPOONS ICE WATER

8 TO 10 APPLES, PEELED,
    CORED, AND SLICED

DIRECTIONS

1. To make the pastry, whisk together the flour, salt, and 1 tablespoon of sugar in a large bowl. Using your fingers, work 6 tablespoons of the butter into the flour mixture until you have coarse clumps. Sprinkle the ice water over the mixture and continue to work it with your hands until the dough just holds together. Shape it into a ball, wrap it in plastic wrap, and refrigerate it for at least 1 hour or overnight.

2. Preparation for the tart starts in a cast-iron skillet. Place the remaining pieces of butter evenly over the bottom of the skillet, then sprinkle the remaining sugar evenly over everything. Next, start placing the apple slices in a circular pattern, starting on the inside edge of the pan working in. The slices should overlap and face the same direction. Place either 1 or 2 slices in the center when finished working around the outside. As the tart bakes, the slices will slide down a bit.

3. Place the skillet on the stove and turn the heat to medium-high. Cook the apples in the pan, uncovered, until the sugar and butter start to caramelize, about 35 minutes. While they're cooking, spoon some of the melted juices over the apples (but don't overdo it).

4. Preheat the oven to 400°F and position a rack in the center.

5. Take the chilled dough out of the refrigerator and, working on a lightly floured surface, roll it out into a circle just big enough to cover the skillet (about 12 to 14 inches). Gently drape the pastry over the apples, tucking it in around the sides. Put the skillet in the oven and bake for about 25 minutes, until the pastry is golden brown. Remove the skillet from the oven and allow to cool for about 5 minutes.

6. Find a plate that is an inch or 2 larger than the top of the skillet and place it over the top. You will be inverting the tart onto the plate. Be sure to use oven mitts or secure pot holders, as the skillet will be hot.

7. Holding the plate tightly against the top of the skillet, turn the skillet over so the plate is now on the bottom. If some of the apples are stuck to the bottom, gently remove them and place them on the tart. Allow to cool for a few more minutes, then serve.

Pumpkin Pecan Tart

YIELD: **6 TO 8 SERVINGS**

ACTIVE TIME: **60 MINUTES**

TOTAL TIME: **1 HOUR AND 30 MINUTES**

In a twist on a traditional pumpkin pie, this tart has the pecans as the crust for a delicious result.

INGREDIENTS

1 ½ CUPS RAW PECANS

1 ½ TABLESPOONS HONEY

2 TABLESPOONS UNSALTED BUTTER, CHILLED AND CUT INTO SMALL PIECES, PLUS 1 TABLESPOON FOR GREASING THE SKILLET

1 (15 OZ.) CAN PUMPKIN PUREE

1 (12 OZ.) CAN EVAPORATED MILK

2 EGGS, LIGHTLY BEATEN

¾ CUP GRANULATED SUGAR

1 TEASPOON GROUND CINNAMON

¼ TEASPOON GROUND GINGER

¼ TEASPOON GROUND ALLSPICE

½ TEASPOON SALT

1 CUP HEAVY CREAM

2 TABLESPOONS CONFECTIONERS' SUGAR

DIRECTIONS

1. Preheat the oven to 400°F.

2. Put the pecans in a food processor and pulse until you have a coarse, crumbly meal. Alternately, you can put the pecans in a large, thick plastic bag and mash them with a rolling pin or meat tenderizer.

3. Transfer the crushed nuts to a bowl and add the honey and butter, mixing with a pastry blender, fork, or your fingers until a coarse meal is formed. There can be chunks of butter.

4. Liberally grease a cast-iron skillet with the butter. Transfer the nut mixture to the skillet and gently press it into the pan to form a crust.

5. Put the skillet on top of a cookie sheet to catch any oil that may spatter. Bake for 10 to 12 minutes, until browned and toasty. Remove from the oven and allow to cool completely on a wire rack.

6. Reduce the oven's temperature to 350°F.

7. In a large bowl, stir together the pumpkin puree and evaporated milk. Add the eggs and stir to combine. Add the sugar, cinnamon, ginger, allspice, and salt and stir to combine thoroughly.

8. Working with the crust in the skillet, transfer the pumpkin mixture into the crust.

9. Put the skillet in the oven and bake for about 50 minutes, until a knife inserted near the center comes out clean. Remove the skillet from the oven and allow to cool completely.

10. Before serving, beat the heavy cream with an electric mixer until soft peaks form. Add the confectioners' sugar 1 tablespoon at a time until it has dissolved and stiff peaks form. Serve the tart with whipped cream.

Peach Galette

YIELD: **6 TO 8 SERVINGS**

ACTIVE TIME: **55 MINUTES**

TOTAL TIME: **3 TO 3 HOURS 30 MINUTES**

When peaches are ripe in the mid-to-late summer, this is a super-simple way to turn them into a great dessert. Smearing some peach jam on the crust before adding the fruit will intensify the flavor.

INGREDIENTS

2 ½ CUPS FLOUR, PLUS MORE
   FOR DUSTING

1 TEASPOON SALT

¼ CUP VEGETABLE SHORTENING

1 STICK BUTTER, CHILLED
   AND CUT INTO SMALL
   PIECES (IF USING UNSALTED
   BUTTER, INCREASE SALT
   TO 1 ¼ TEASPOONS), PLUS 1
   TABLESPOON FOR GREASING
   THE SKILLET

6 TO 8 TABLESPOONS COLD WATER

3 CUPS FRESH PEACHES, PEELED,
   PITTED, AND SLICED

½ CUP SUGAR, PLUS 1 TABLESPOON

JUICE OF ½ LEMON

3 TABLESPOONS CORNSTARCH

PINCH OF SALT

2 TABLESPOONS PEACH JAM

1 TEASPOON AMARETTO LIQUEUR
   (OPTIONAL)

1 EGG, BEATEN

RASPBERRIES, FOR GARNISH
   (OPTIONAL)

DIRECTIONS

1. In a large bowl, combine the flour and salt. Add the shortening and, using a fork, work it in until the mixture forms a very coarse meal. Add the stick of butter and work into the dough with a pastry blender or your fingers until the dough is just holding together. Don't overwork the dough.

2. Add 4 tablespoons cold water to start and, using your hands or a fork, work the dough, adding additional tablespoons of water until the dough just holds together when you gather it in your hands.

3. Working on a lightly floured surface, gather the dough and form it into a solid ball. Wrap tightly in plastic wrap and refrigerate for 30 to 60 minutes.

4. Take the dough out of the refrigerator to allow it to warm up slightly. While still cold, place the refrigerated dough on a lightly floured surface and flatten with a floured rolling pin, working both sides to extend each into a 9- to 12-inch round.

5. Grease a cast-iron skillet with 1 tablespoon of butter. Carefully position the crust in the skillet so it is evenly distributed, pressing it in lightly and allowing the dough to extend over the side. The crust in the skillet should be slightly larger than the bottom of the pan so that it can be folded over.

Continued on next page...

6. Preheat oven to 400°F. In a large bowl, mix the peaches with the ½ cup of sugar, lemon juice, cornstarch, and salt. Stir well to be sure to coat all the fruit.

7. If using the liqueur, mix it with the jam in a small bowl before smearing the jam on the center of the crust.

8. Place the fruit in a mound in the center of the crust. Fold the edge of the crust over to cover about 1 inch of filling. Brush the crust with the beaten egg and sprinkle it with the remaining sugar.

9. Put the skillet in the oven and bake until the filling is bubbly, which is necessary for it to thicken sufficiently, about 35 to 40 minutes.

10. Remove the skillet from the oven and allow to cool. If using, garnish with raspberries before serving.

ABOUT THE AUTHOR

❧

KIMBERLY STEVENS is a seasoned writer and journalist who has contributed extensively to *The New York Times* and written stories for *The Los Angeles Times*, *The Wall Street Journal*, numerous national magazines, and online publications. Her spare time finds her battling a severe addiction to cookbook collecting, shopping at the farmer's market, and making meals for friends and family.

ABOUT CIDER MILL PRESS
BOOK PUBLISHERS

❧

Good ideas ripen with time. From seed to harvest,
Cider Mill Press brings fine reading, information,
and entertainment together between the covers of its
creatively crafted books. Our Cider Mill bears fruit twice
a year, publishing a new crop of titles each spring and fall.

CIDER MILL
PRESS

BOOK
PUBLISHERS
KENNEBUNKPORT, MAINE

"Where Good Books Are Ready for Press"

Visit us online at
cidermillpress.com
or write to us at
PO Box 454
12 Spring St.
Kennebunkport, Maine 04046

SAVOR IMAGE CREDITS

All hand lettering and illustrations by Victoria Black.

INDEX